Homeopathy for Home

Acute Illness and Injury Care

Homeopathy for Home

Acute Illness & Injury Care

Kim Lane, MD

To order additional copies of this book, contact:
Xlibris Corporation
1-888-795-4274
www.Xlibris.com
Orders@Xlibris.com
103583

Contents

Lovingly dedicated to LRM.

Preface

This is my first book. It is an attempt to record what, hopefully, will be useful information for any person to use in their self-care using homeopathy. I had found so few books that were inclusive of the aspects I have chosen here to present.

The first section on the substance and theory of homeopathy is a very small glimpse, an attempt to help the reader perhaps understand a bit of the science behind the workings of homeopathy as defined by Samuel Hahnemann. There are other books that deal with this more in depth. My goal was to introduce you, the reader, to some terms and ideas to assist you in your use of homeopathy on a personal level.

The next sections on acute illness and first aid offer assistance to the reader to take care of themselves or their family without needing to use other modalities in a safe and effective way. Again, this work is but a brief group of remedies that may be used in an acute fashion to assist in return to health. They will not remove the need for allopathic care when it is necessary.

The surgical section is an added portion to this work. I have found in my patients, as they use it, that they recover faster and often surprise the surgeon with their remarkable healing. So I included it here, should you have the need.

I have been an allopathic family physician for twenty-five years now, and I am also certified in holistic medicine. I found that there were people I could not help. I also found that it seemed I would have to give a prescription for the side effects of another prescription previously written. I found, in homeopathy, a way to help folks get better and not need so many prescriptions. My goal, as a medical provider, is that my patients would heal and not need me. A holistic approach to health along with homeopathy has helped that happen.

I opened Wellness Lane, LLC in 2007 to make classical homeopathy, wellness consultation, and homeopathy education a personal and professional focus. "We bring good health to life" guides our mission. *Homeopathy for Home is a part of this mission.*

With this book, it is my hope that I share some of that knowledge that you can use for yourself and your family.

There are many ways to health—diet, exercise, acupuncture, chiropractic, homeopathy, allopathy, energy work, naturopathy, medicines, herbal treatments, prayer. There is not one way. May you find the care you need for an abundance of health.

Kim Lane, MD
Wellness Lane, LLC
2010

Acknowledgments

First, I would like to thank my family—Linda Metzger for her invaluable and necessary assistance in typing and editing this book; my children, Maria and Emma, for the time this has taken that I could not spend with them.

I would like to thank my teachers at the Northwestern Academy of Homeopathy—Val Ohanian, Laurie Dack, and Eric Sommermann for the basis of my knowledge and the instruction to think more deeply. Also, Dr. Rajan Sankaran for his thought-provoking and enlightening instruction in "Wednesdays with Rajan."

I would like to thank Michele Brookhaus, mentor extraordinaire, and the members of the Minnesota Homeopathic Association executive board, who continue to offer support and time to stretch my abilities.

Thank you to my allopathic colleagues, Bill Manahan, MD, and Karen Vrchota, MD, and the members of the Minnesota Holistic Medical Association for their example, support, and encouragement to expand healing beyond the traditional.

I must thank Tina Rosenquist, *Knowledge for Wellness* producer and editor, for her excellent assistance and expertise to edit and produce the DVD portion of this work. If DVDs are not included with your book; they may be ordered through www.wellnesslane.us.

A special thank you to the folks at Xlibris for their expertise in editing, designing and bringing this book to print.

I would finally like to thank those students who have lived through this course and offered their worthwhile suggestions and my patients for their trust in the wonderful healing process of homeopathy.

Introduction to Homeopathy

Homeopathy for Home Series

(If included, please insert disc 1: Introduction to Homeopathy.)

We will cover the following areas:

1. Introduction of what homeopathy is and about the father of homeopathy
2. The Law of Similars
3. The direction of disease and its cure
4. Terminology
5. Remedies—what are they?
6. Dosing and homeopathy
7. Acute versus chronic treatment
8. How does it work?

The Father of Homeopathy

Samuel Hahnemann, MD (1755-1843), is the father of homeopathy. He studied all the local healers and was actually fluent in six different languages. He was a physician of his time and realized that bloodletting and giving mercury for syphilis were not effective in bringing his patients to health. In studying the other healers, herbalists, and some of the works of Aristotle, he defined the homeopathic principle. He wrote all his work in a book called the *Organon of the Medical Art*. He completed five editions, which were published while he was alive. The sixth was published by his wife after he died. There are many translations of the *Organon of the Medical Art*.

Homeopathy: Its Beginnings

Homeopathy is a deep and gentle healing. It works on the whole person. Hahnemann propagated the *law of similars* on which homeopathy is based. He did this through the observation of cinchona, also called Peruvian bark. Cinchona was actually used by the Peruvian Indians for the treatment of malaria. Dr. Hahnemann observed cinchona after he had diluted and energized it and noticed that it caused similar symptoms to malaria. And in doing this and proving it several times, he realized that the energy of cinchona, which was used to treat malaria, actually caused similar symptoms of malaria in healthy people. As he studied several other remedies, he found similar responses. He then put together *Organon of the Medical Art*.

The *Organon of the Medical Art* is rather like the Bible/Koran/how-to manual for homeopathy. The *Organon* tells how to take a case from a patient, how to evaluate, and then how to choose a remedy. It also tells how to prepare a remedy and how to treat a patient. It has very explicit information.

The Law of Similars

The Law of Similars is "like treats like," similia similibus curantur. This, again, uses a very different methodology than we are used to here in the United States. The Law of Similars is this: if the remedy in the healthy gives the same symptoms for an illness that the patient has, then that remedy is chosen to treat that patient.

This is very different from our allopathic medicines, which most of us here in our country grew up with and which is the law of opposites. For instance, if we have high blood pressure, we will give something to lower blood pressure. If we have a high blood sugar, we will give something to lower blood sugar. But in allopathic medicine, we give something to only treat the high blood pressure and high sugar. Whereas in homeopathy, we look at the whole person, and we would give them something that in a healthy person would give them high blood pressure because it's the energy of the substance that helps the body return to health. This hopefully will become clearer as you continue.

Illness or Disease

Illness or disease is caused by a stress to the body. And actually, both allopaths and homeopaths would agree to that. The best book that I read that was most understandable was *The Science of Homeopathy* by George Vithoulkas. This book was written by a Greek homeopath who is still practicing today, and he gives an excellent explanation of homeopathy that is worth reading. It talks about what homeopathy is, the theory behind it, how to evaluate if a remedy is working or not. It is well written and much easier to read, I think, than the *Organon of the Medical Art.*

Levels of Disease—The other thing about illness and homeopathy is that it is looked at in three different levels: the physical, the emotional, and the mental. The physical, being the most superficial; the deeper level, being the emotional; and then we go up to the mental. So if you are ill or if your illness is suppressed, it will go deeper. For instance, in homeopathy, we look at eczema in babies as being a significant illness, and if suppressed with steroids and other creams, often we'll see that it will go into asthma. If the asthma is suppressed also with other medications and steroids, it will progress to anxiety and depression. The eczema progressed from superficial physical to deeper physical (lungs) to emotional levels.

As an allopathic physician, this child would be called an atopic child. As an allopath, I then would expect to see the eczema go to asthma. As a physician, I hadn't noted, until I studied homeopathy, that anxiety and depression followed, but I have seen that in folks who have those allergies in their early twenties and thirties have some anxiety and depression. So we've gone from the physical to the emotional to the mental level in the different depth of the physical disease, which we'll talk about more in a little bit.

Disease—A disease can be caused in homeopathy by a cold wind, exposure to a germ—which allopaths would agree—grief, or an injury, which again would follow well with our allopathic traditions here in the United States. Now, how the body responds to or reacts to this cold wind or germ or grief or injury is the illness. If one does not react, there is no illness.

In homeopathy, disease which is more superficial is less severe. An allopath would agree with that. So skin disease is usually less life threatening than heart attack or a brain injury, for example. Disease is more superficial in the physical realm going deeper as it progresses to the emotional level becoming most significant at the mental level.

Susceptibility—Vital Force and Miasm

The other piece about disease and homeopathy that is important is the vital force strength, and the general susceptibility of a person (which Hahnemann defined such susceptibility as miasm) will affect the degree of illness. An example of this might be that you get chilled and perhaps you get a sore throat. Somebody else gets a cough, somebody else gets a stomach upset, somebody else gets a headache. All those are different susceptibilities, and depending on what's seen, we have ways to classify and look at that person's reactions, so that better helps us select, as a homeopath, the remedy that will best help them. There will be more on these areas later.

Direction of Cure

Disease travels to the center—from the outside into the center and then up. Cure will travel, according to *Hering's law*, toward the periphery and down. As you get sick, it goes from the outside in and from the bottom up, and as you start to cure and as we see healing, we will see things heal from the inside out and from the top down. The body will choose what is most significant to heal.

Also in homeopathy, we will notice that the symptoms that were most recent will go away first usually, and then the ones that were earlier will go away last. Again, the body, in its wisdom, will choose what affects it most and try to rebalance in the best way for maximum health and function.

Hering's Law

Cure proceeds from above downward, from within outward, from the most important organ to the least important organ, and in the reverse order of the appearance of symptoms.
Now we're going to talk about some books that are in homeopathy and continue on with terminology.

Terminology and Books

Books

The *Organon* is the book of homeopathy and has all the information on how to make a remedy, on how to take a case, how to evaluate if the patient is indeed improving.

The *Materia Medica* is a book of each remedy and what it does in the proving. So the *Materia Medica* is a summary of the remedy and everything it affects through the systems in the body. So if you look up Arnica Montana, you will have everything that Arnica Montana affects. Now there are many *Materia Medicas*, and some are easily understood, some are more complete than other, and some are just more favored than others by how you were trained. This is not unlike when going to medical school, there are certain books, like Harriet Lane, for pediatric information that I would choose and prefer.

The *Repertory* is a book of all symptoms by location. So we start out with the mind, the head, the throat, the chest, the extremities, the stomach, the abdomen, and general symptoms; and in the *Repertory*, we have the symptoms grouped under each organ system, and then remedies are listed under it. All the remedies for head pain from cold will be under that particular location, which is actually called the *rubric*.

There are also several *computer programs*. *MacRep*, which was originally made in California to work on Macintosh machines, but both of the computer programs work on PCs or Macs or Apples. *Radar* came out of the Netherlands. These have many Materia Medicas and many Repertories, and the nice thing about the computer program is that it can sort through all those and saves the homeopath many hours in searching for a remedy.

Terminology

Vital force—It is the energy of health and life. It is different from the soul. It is probably the same as kundalini or qi that are used in other healing methodologies. The vital force is probably between the soul and the heart and breathing. It's an energy that has been noted. This is the level where the remedy will act.

Provings—They are how a remedy is tested before it is used. Provings are all done on healthy people. Hahnemann had a very strong belief that we should first do no harm, the Hippocratic oath, and so he would not test remedies on people who were sick. So provings are given usually in a fairly low dose, 30C for a number of days, sometimes just three days until the symptoms are noticed. The prover will have a person (scribe or observer) they talk to every day and who will document all their symptoms, dreams, what they thought, their cravings, and these are all collated. The proving will last up to eight weeks, and these are all collated, and the similarities are used, or anything that is really peculiar is used as part of what the remedy will work on.

All the characteristic symptoms will be organized into the repertory of each of the symptom areas. The proving is written as a new addition to the Materia Medica, which was that particular substance and all that it affects. Provings have been invaluable, and they're quite incredible when we participated in school. They are often done at conferences so we can develop new remedies. So every remedy in homeopathy has been proven on healthy people, and we know what it does, which is a remarkable thing.

Succussion—It is a means of energizing, and it's done in each dilution. It is also called potentization. First dilution is made if it's solid, 1 gram of the substance with 9 grams usually of sucrose and milk sugar or lactose, and then it is diluted, and every dilution of 10 gets succussed 20 to 40 times. Succussion means using the remedy in a flask and hitting it against something that won't break the flask. It's not shaking. Shaking is random; succussion is direct energy to the substance. Like taking your fist and pounding it one hundred times on a telephone book would be succussion if you had a flask in it.

Dosage or potency—The dosage or potency is how we define the energy of the remedy. It's the dilution of the remedy. The more diluted the remedy, the deeper the action. This is directly opposite of our allopathic doses where more drug is more action or more side effects and where we hope those side effects are good side effects. We will talk more specifically about dosage at a later time.

Keynotes—They are a symptom so striking that it strongly suggests or points to a single or specific remedy. For example, a keynote for Chelidonium is pain under the right shoulder blade, right at the base of it, at the apex. Another one is for a sore throat where liquids are worse than solids. And that's Lachesis, which happens to be a snake, and if you think about snakes, they swallow food whole. They don't drink either. They just swallow it right down, which is very interesting. So keynotes are something that when we hear certain symptoms, we will think immediately of a remedy that we've known and studied. And as a homeopath, when I'm studying a case, I like to see a few keynotes in the case that confirm the chosen remedy and help me know that it is the right remedy for the patient.

Nosodes—They are potentized remedies prepared from diseased tissue. There's a nosode in each of miasms, which we'll talk about in the next paragraph. Psorinum, the itch or scabies, is for psoric miasm, Medorrhinum is for the sycotic miasm, and Syphilinum is for the syphilitic miasm. Nosodes are used in homeopathy when we can see definitely that a patient fits a certain disease susceptibility miasm, and their symptoms don't lead you to a specific remedy within that category.

Miasms—Hahnemann's definition of miasms is "a noxious influence and is the infectious principle or virus, which when taken into the organism, may set up a specific disease." Now, to Hahnemann, virus just meant germ since they didn't know viruses in his time, and the microscope in his time would not have been able to visualize viruses. Miasms are used to help us choose a remedy that fits best with all the symptoms that we see. So in addition to the principle miasms of psora, sycotic, and syphilitic, which I mentioned in the nosodes in the above paragraph, we have an acute miasm, tubercular miasm, typhoid miasm, malarial miasm, ringworm miasm, leprosy miasm, and cancerous miasm. Except for the acute miasm, these have all been added since Hahnemann's time, and we use these because there are certain characteristics we look for in a patient's symptoms that fit well into these categories.

Miasms

I'm going to talk about the different miasms and what they mean. For me, miasms are a bit like family history in the allopathic sense. They do correlate a bit in that regard, and we can, in fact, inherit a miasm from our parents or grandparents or someone in the family, or we can inherit a miasm because of what happened to our mom while we were in the womb. So let me start with defining the first miasm, the acute miasm.

Acute miasm—There is a strong feeling of a threat from the outside world, and the reaction is instinctive, strong, and reflexive. If you think about getting hit by a car, that's an acute incident. There's no preparation for it; it just happens. Homeopathically, we can treat in the acute sense. First aid treatment or treatment of acute illness may be treated with a small group of remedies. If we're treating someone constitutionally in the acute miasm, then we look for something that put them in that place. We also know that their sense of response is going to be reflexive and instinctive and strong, and it will just happen. Constitutionally, posttraumatic stress folks might fit in the acute miasm because usually their disease results from their being attacked, frightened, or a traumatic acute event resulting in reflexive and persistent symptoms. For constitutional homeopathic care, again, we have to know the specifics of each person we talk to. The acute miasm that will be covered here will be in relation to acute injury and acute illness.

Psoric miasm—Psora has a sense of a great struggle to succeed; there's an outside stressor, and there's a doubt about the ability to succeed, but there is hope, and failure's not the end of the world. Usually, there's a hypersensitivity, there's periodicity (where the symptoms come and go), there are usually skin symptoms, an anxiety. People in the psoric miasms tend to be better with cold, they're better at night, and they tend to be energy-giving people. And if you think about scabies or know about anyone who has, it really is quite irritating—you itch, you feel not quite good enough with the scabies, like they attacked you and they spread—but you know that you won't die from scabies. And you know that, eventually, they'll go away. That's the psoric sense of great struggle, but they're very hopeful, and the scabies will itch here and there, and there are usually rashes noted in the psoric miasm.

Sycotic miasm—Sycosis is "the sense of I am not capable of handling this situation, something is wrong with me." And they will try to cope by covering it up. There's a lot of secrecy, there's an ego, and there are compulsive acts with the person who's in the sycotic miasm. The patient will have a sense that there is no likelihood of complete recovery. Usually, we'll see hypertrophy or overgrowth, we'll see water retention, we'll see warty growths, we'll see obsessions. These folks are worse from cold damp weather; they're worse at night. They have a repugnant sort of energy. The nosode for this is Medorrhinum, which is gonorrhea. What helped me remember the miasms is to remember the nosodes; as a physician, knowing the disease and what it was like was a helpful piece. If you think about having gonorrhea, it's not something that one would announce to the world. In fact, there's a kind of a bit of secrecy, shame about it, a feeling of "I did something wrong," and you want to cover it up, and you feel like you're dirty forever. Often, the other thing associated with sycotic miasm is overgrowths, like venereal warts. Gonorrhea is repugnant, so if you consider the disease and think about the miasm, the characteristics of the disease remind one of the miasm characteristics.

Syphilitic miasm—The person in this miasm will be "faced with a situation beyond salvage, complete hopelessness, and despair." There's a giving up here. Therefore, they will often do a drastic do-or-die attempt to change themselves or their environment so they can survive. Symptomwise, we will see destructive or degenerative symptoms, more severe phobias and anxieties, insomnia, and bony deformities. In the syphilitic miasm, one would see rheumatoid or osteoarthritis with destructive bony lesions where the joint's destroyed. (The sycotic miasm form of osteoarthritis or rheumatoid arthritis would be bony joint overgrowth where we have a lot of knobs and swelling of the joints.) The syphilitic miasm is also worse at night. This is an energy-taking person. They are really at the end stage of life, and it is a very significant and difficult place to be for a person who is in this miasm. Now these four miasms—the acute, the psoric, the sycotic, and the syphilitic—are all miasms of Hahnemann's time and ones he dealt with during his lifetime. Now we have some newer miasms.

Typhoid miasm—This is also called the *subacute*. Here, this is an intense struggle, an acute threat from the outside, and there's a feeling though of a critical situation, but if it's handled properly in the critical period, all will end well. If you think about typhoid fever, which is the nosode for this miasm, typhoid comes with an acute gut reaction (perhaps you are aware of Typhoid Mary), lots of diarrhea with the potential for dehydration and death. Most typhoid is self-limiting and will eventually go away, and no treatment is given. Allopathically, with typhoid, we do not treat with antibiotics unless symptoms persist because most folks are better in about a week or so. One must maintain hydration and rest, of course. So the typhoid miasm is subacute because if you get dehydrated, you can die. Some people are so sensitive they can get bloody diarrhea. Not a fun illness to have.

Malarial miasm—This person would feel an acute threat and a sense of chronic deficiency. There's a sense of persecution that also happens in the malarial miasm. There's a periodicity to it—it will come and go. If you know about malaria, there are the tertian malarial incidences coming every three or four days where there will be a period that one will feel well and then one will feel ill. But one never knows when this will happen. There is also the sense of persecution that comes with malaria. If you think of how one gets malaria, it's the mosquito, and if there's one insect that can certainly make you feel like you're being persecuted, it is a swarm of mosquitoes. So that's one way of remembering the malarial miasm. Malaria is the nosode for the malarial miasm.

Ringworm miasm—With ringworm, there's a struggle with anxiety about success, and there's a fixity to it; there's a feeling of inadequacy with oneself. The difficult situation is just beyond easy reach. One doubts that they can succeed. But there's a hope that alternates a little bit with giving up. But it's not fatal. If you think about ringworm, it's a rash, it looks ugly, it's fixed (meaning, well-defined edges). It just grows bigger. Most people that have it feel like it's taking over their body and feel pretty ugly, but it's not like they'll die. It's just rather irritating. So there's a struggle, and they have this rash, and they think it'll go away. The ringworm miasm is quite like that.

Tubercular miasm—This has a sense of oppression, as if one's weakness is being exploited and they need to take a deep breath. There's also a sense of suffocation, and if you think about tuberculosis, it's usually a disease of the lungs; there is a sense of suffocation especially at the end, and there is a continuing sense of weakness. It's destructive at times, causing cavitary lesions. There is a desperateness that one wants to break free but can't, and they can't breathe. The other thing I want to say that helps me remember the characteristic of the miasm is to think about what happened with tuberculosis. When I grew up, there were sanitariums where people with TB were left for months to years to try to recover so they wouldn't share the disease with their family. But they had to leave everything and just stay in those places away from everybody else. They also would be sent to the mountains or the seashore for the clean fresh air, which seemed to help heal tuberculosis. So people of the tubercular miasm actually do love to travel, especially to mountains and seashore. Usually, respiratory illness is frequent with that sense of suffocation or oppression.

Leprosy miasm—Leprosy is an old disease, and those people in this miasm usually have a sense of intense hopelessness and depression. They really want to change, but they have self-loathing, and certainly there's a destructive nature/feeling to this miasm. The leprosy miasm—if you think of the nosode, leprosy—causes a lack of feeling in the fingers, nose, toes, and distal areas. So these numb areas are easily injured, get infected, necrose (die), and fall off. You recall that lepers were also sent away as outcasts to the leper colonies and could never see their families again. Leprosy still exists in our country in the southern United States and around the world. This miasm has gone on through generations with this sense of being outcasts and the destruction that goes along with that. It's pretty much a miasm of despair, quite close to syphilis, not quite as hopeless or suicidal as syphilis miasm.

Cancer miasm—People in the cancer miasm experience the stress of the need to perform well. They want to live up to expectations, but there's a feeling of weakness within. They need to do this with superhuman effort, and they want to be perfect. There's chaos around them, and they want control over it. They're asked often in their early growing-up years to do more than they can do; or even as adults, this sometimes can come on. So there's a real sense of being unable to do all that needs to be done. There's also destruction and overgrowth in this miasm when you look at the physical problems. Carcinosin is the nosode for the cancer miasm.

The miasms are all related in a circular fashion with acute to psoric to sycotic to syphilitic, and these miasms can be seen on your slide series.

We have some more terminologies now, stepping away from miasms.

Terminology of Treatment

There's also the **acute illness**. An acute illness is one that is recent. It's usually treated with a lower potency, and it's a first aid treatment. So an acute illness would be the sore throat or earache that just all of a sudden came or could be an acute injury like a broken bone. It's not been around for a long time. And the first aid treatment (you'll know by the end the first aid treatments so you can treat acutely) is done where you don't need to do a whole constitutional evaluation; there are few things to know and ask, and you can choose the remedy that will best fit the symptoms the patient is having.

Chronic or constitutional treatment—Now this requires a formal evaluation by a homeopath. We use higher doses, and we look more at the whole person. In the chronic or constitutional treatment, we'll be looking back over something that someone's had for months or years. So it's not that they just got it and had it for an hour or two or a few days. This is something that's been bothering them and is persisting. They will need different doses. It's not a first aid treatment. One must study the case and look at all the rubrics and symptoms in the *Repertory* and then study the *Materia Medica* and see if things line up well with the symptoms and characteristics the patient brings.

Suppression—Suppression, in homeopathic terminology, is something that works against the healing and the vital force. So suppression might be taking a steroid medication because that turns off the immune system and the body can't rebalance. It may be taking a medicine for a cold. Colds, in homeopathy, are often seen as a rebalancing for the vital force. When one is stressed often, a cold or viral illness results. If we were wise in our culture, we would take time off and drink our fluids and rest. But instead, we take some medicines and go to work and continue moving on. So the suppression can actually make us more ill. Suppression usually will drive whatever is going on in our system deeper, which is not, as a homeopath, preferred.

Aggravation—Aggravation is a flare-up of known symptoms; it's usually short-lived, and occurs after taking a remedy. Sometimes, a remedy is just too strong for a patient if they're very sensitive. To the homeopath, an aggravation is reassuring that a good remedy was chosen, but it's not fun for the patient. So it means an adjustment of dose—either plussing it or giving a different dosage level altogether. An aggravation is usually short-lived—only a few days, and depending on the remedy dose, it might just be one day to one week. If aggravations are severe or causing major issues, then one should certainly contact their homeopath who prescribed the remedy because there are things to do to decrease the aggravations.

Remedy—Remedy is the substance we use for healing in homeopathy. Remedies are anything from the earth and around the earth, from minerals to plants and to animals, the milks of animals to insects. The herbalists often believe that within a mile of their house lives every herb that you need to maintain your health. What's interesting to me, for many of us, there are a lot of dandelions around the house, at least in my suburb, and I think about that because dandelions are a great liver purifier, and we really have a lot of toxins in our environment with how we've chosen to eat and live. (Our liver is the organ of detoxification.) We will talk about remedies more and give some examples as we get into the acute and first aid treatments.

Remedies are anything on the earth as I said before. They are diluted and succussed, which is energized before they're used. It's the energy of the substance, not the substance itself. The more diluted the dose, the deeper the healing for a remedy. And remember, the characteristics for each remedy are noted in *Materia Medica*, and the symptoms for a particular remedy are in the *Repertory*.

Remedy strength—Dilution—X is one over 10; C is one over 100; M is one over 1,000 C. Now, note X, C, and M are the roman numerals for 10, 100, and 1,000, respectively. So if you know those, it'll help. One C (1C) is equal to one over a hundred to the first power. A two C (2C) is equal to one over the second power or one over 10,000. Often, for acute remedies, we give a 30C, so that's one of a hundred to the 30th power $(1/100^{30})$.

The remedy strength is also related to the remedy potentization and succussion, which is a vigorous pounding on a thick book between each dilution. There are a certain number of times that one must succuss—100 times for each dilution. The preparation is well defined in the *Organon of the Medical Art* by Samuel Hahnemann (see preparation of medicines aphorisms 264-271).

An **LM** is a 1/50,000 solution (LM1= $1/50,000^1$, LM3= $1/50,000^3$). It's liquid, and usually one takes seven drops in a quarter cup of filtered or distilled water, stirs it ten times, and takes one teaspoon of that remedy daily most of the time. The number of drops can be increased or decreased. This is a remedy that's given as a constitutional remedy prescribed by a homeopath. It's usually given to someone who is either very frail or very sensitive or someone on many medications, and we don't want to put them into a severe aggravation because if you stop the LM, the aggravation goes away within a day. One can finely adjust how much of the remedy is being given according to the patient.

Potency—The higher the dilution, the deeper acting the remedy. So a 30C will work on an acute injury that is short-lived and has since worked its way down into the deeper organs—perhaps the brain or the mental, emotional area. Because homeopathic remedies are an energy medicine, one is able to take two pellets or a hundred pellets and will get the same identical dose. Of course, if you take 100 pellets, your bottle of remedy won't last as long, so that's not advised.

The other thing about remedies and potency is that there is no material dose or material substance in dilutions of more than 23X $(1/10^{23})$ or 12C $(1/100^{12})$. So there's purely energy but *no* material substance of the original remedy. Some folks say that homeopathy is just placebo effect; however, I've seen it work on dogs and babies. It's very hard for dogs or babies to have a placebo effect since they don't have the intellect to know what we're doing for them. Homeopathic provings and looking at the effects of our remedies over the years gives us the information to know how each remedy works. It's amazing how through homeopathy, the energy of a substance works so well.

Homeopathic Theory

So what is the theory behind homeopathy? The energy of the remedy tweaks the vital force to begin healing. My belief is that because the energy of the remedy is similar to the symptoms the patient is having and giving them that remedy, the vital force notices it. "Oh, okay, I'm going to rebalance, so that's not bothering me," says the vital force, and then the body begins to heal. This is a simple explanation for a sophisticated idea. *The Science of Homeopathy* by George Vithoulkas has some good explanations on the theory of homeopathy and may be of interest to you.

Remedy dispensing and care—Since it is energy medicine, avoid placing the pills on your hand, take it using the cap, or use a metal spoon to dispense. If diluting a remedy, mix it in glass container, or if you use plastic, it must be virgin plastic (a plastic that's never been used). Plastic will retain the energy and, sometimes, material for whatever it had contact with before and therefore risks adding a different energy. So you do not want to lose the energy or transfer unwanted energy into your dose at the time you take it. For diluting that will give a plussed dose, it is best to use bottled, filtered, or distilled water.

The healing energy of the remedy can be affected by other energies such as strong odors, drugs, caffeine, alcohol, marijuana, spicy foods, x-ray, and of course, sunlight—if it's exposed to sunlight and not covered. Any extreme temperatures, whether extremely hot or extremely cold, will affect the potency of the remedy. So you want to take care to not store your remedy near the spice cabinet or near the Vicks. And try not to use other drugs or medications when you take the remedy. The other rule is not to take anything by mouth 15 minutes before and after you take the remedy if you can. For acute first aid treatment, you give the remedy right away and just repeat as needed.

Dosing—Dosing for homeopathy is different from allopathic dosing. For an acute injury, it's usually 30C ($1/100^{30}$). We can use that dose because it is a short-lived symptom and usually not too deep into a person's being or affecting the vital force in a significant way. Now if there's a significant severe injury, that is not always true. For constitutional dosing, we use a 200C or LMs, and a trained homeopath would prescribe these doses.

If someone is very infirmed or like a small pet, then for 6 times, a 6C or 12C is given. Less vitality uses smaller doses, or if it is a really small animal, use a smaller dose. In babies and humans, usually 30C is well tolerated. Actually, babies quite often have a strong vital force and may even tolerate a 200C or 1M right off the bat. It depends again what their symptoms are and what's happening.

Another consideration about dosing is if it's *very severe or life threatening,* give whatever you can give—200C or 1M—especially if there's a head injury or concussion or any neurological issue that's significant in that they could die; you give whatever you have, and if you have a higher dose, it might help them heal and continue to live.

An important guideline about dosing is that *you do not give the same dose more than once,* according to Hahnemann. That's one of our guiding rules, and it's really important to not do that. If you repeat a dose too often, you can cause proving symptoms to happen, which is different from an aggravation in that they're new symptoms and they're symptoms from the remedy not because the patient is healing. Interestingly, giving the same dose 2, 3, or 4 times in a twenty-four-hour period is almost the same as giving a single dose, so it doesn't really seem to matter as much. Giving the same dose for days in a row can cause proving symptoms. One must pay attention to the symptoms and stop when better. There is also a way to change the dose called plussing.

Plussing is placing 2 to 5 pellets in 2 to 4 ounces of filtered, distilled, or spring water with no minerals or carbonation. Stir 10 times with a metal spoon and take 1 teaspoon per dose. This mixture must be kept in the dark, and each time you take a dose, you stir it 10 times and take 1 teaspoon as directed. Stirring changes the dosage each time because stirring is energizing. This gives a more potentized dose each time, and a plussed remedy will last about twenty-four hours longer if it's preserved with a little alcohol, again depending how it's kept. Plussing is used quite frequently in a patient who's quite sensitive or has an acute problem happening or needs to change his dose or need to take it over several days. It's a great way to give the remedy. Also, it works well if you don't have much of the remedy because, with a quarter to a half cup of water, you can treat many people from the same remedy. And that's especially nice for something like the influenza where the whole family is exposed and sick. This will be discussed more at a later time.

Frequency of dosing—How often or what's the frequency? Acutely, it depends on severity. If it's of a life-threatening nature, it's given every 5, 15, to 30, 60 minutes. Or if it's not so acute or life threatening and symptoms tolerate, 3 to 4 times a day. So basically, remedies are given to help the symptoms. So if the symptoms resolve, you stop the remedy. This avoids aggravation and exacerbation of the symptoms. Proving symptoms will occur if you keep giving it. Unlike antibiotics where you take them 3 times a day for 10 days, with homeopathy, you take it as directed, stopping when symptoms have improved. If symptoms return, you just take another dose. The other thing about homeopathy is less is more and better, which is why you stop when you're better. So one really pays more attention to the symptoms and what's happening for the person you are treating.

Homeopathy will not supplant the need for appropriate emergency room or allopathic treatment. A remedy will help in the healing. It will not set a bone. It will not remove an appendix. It will not give oxygen or give fluids. It will not sew up a laceration. So you need to take/send people to the appropriate care area or emergency room, urgent care, or doctor's office. Homeopathy can definitely be used along with other allopathic treatment. There are some caveats on timing some of which will be discussed. Seek out your homeopathic professional for specific cases and questions.

If you're listening to DVD, stop and consider answering the questions for review.

Review Quiz

1. Briefly, what is the theory of homeopathy?
2. Describe what a homeopathic remedy is.
3. In homeopathy, we talk of miasm. How would you describe what a miasm is?
4. Who is the father/founder of homeopathy?
5. Define disease.
6. What is a 30C potency? Ten times?
7. Why is succussion used?

(Answers are on page 75.)

Homeopathy for Acute Illness

(If included, please insert disk 2: Homeopathy for Acute Illness)

We will cover the following areas:
- A brief review of the theory of homeopathy
- The infections, which include cough and influenza
- Sore throats, earaches, urinary tract infections
- Summary

Homeopathic Guide Rules

Remember the following:

- Symptoms matter—*like treats like*. This is very important to consider in homeopathy.
- A little remedy goes a long way in homeopathy. It's an *energy* medicine, *so less is more; dose* depends on the patient and the situation.
- *Dosing frequency* will depend on the severity of the illness and on the strength of the vital force. So if someone is pretty infirm, less is usually recommended. If it's very severe and life threatening, then you give what you have and you may give more of a higher dose, which is more diluted and more energetic and less material substance. If one is on a constitutional remedy, remember to consult your homeopath, or the homeopath of the person being treated for the remedy you're on constitutionally may cover your acute situation.
- *Plussing* is placing 1 to 3 pellets in a quarter to a half cup of filtered or distilled water and then stirring 10 times and taking 1 teaspoon. This is done in a glass container and kept in the dark so the energy is not dispersed. This allows both variation of the dose and increasing the dose with each time it's taken. So one would stir then 10 times

for the next dose and repeat as directed for the situation that you are treating.

- *Seek medical care when needed.* Homeopathy will not cover all the situations that will present themselves, and sometimes, you need more than homeopathy; you need allopathic remedies, say for IV fluids and significant situations.

Respiratory Infections

Colds or upper respiratory infections—If the vital force or the person's energy is fine, no treatment is really necessary. Colds and respiratory infections are an excellent way the body rebalances itself from stressors, and you can tell it's a rebalance because your energy will basically be pretty good. Pay attention to that. That doesn't mean you work out hard and continue with a normal schedule during this illness or in a stressful time, but you do need to take some care. Stay well hydrated and get some rest and eat appropriate foods to care for your body and help it pass through this rebalancing time.

If one is on a constitutional remedy and just had a new dose or a new remedy, this may be a healing response, especially if the vital force is good. The other thing I would say, if you have a cold from a constitutional remedy, what you will also notice is the symptoms will move quickly, changing rapidly all the while you feel pretty good about them, so you may have a sore throat for a half a day or even a few hours, instead of twenty-four hours, and it goes to congestion of the nose and then maybe to a cough, but it all moves out of your system fairly quickly; and certainly, it will be less significant than the usual cold, which now last seven to fourteen days for most people.

Remedies for Coughs

Aconite—The person who needs this remedy will be in the early stages of a cough; they'll have a recent exposure to a cold, dry wind, a very significant and very much associated precondition with Aconite. Almost any illness that occurs after a cold, dry wind, consider Aconite. These folks will feel worse at night; they'll feel worse when they sleep. They will be better lying on their back. They are usually highly anxious, fearful, or restless folks especially when they are ill. So look for those characteristics when you're thinking of giving a person Aconite.

Arsenicosum—These folks will have a thin, watery, burning discharge. Arsenicosum usually has burning and it's discharge is usually watery. This remedy could treat a congestion from allergy or infection. These folks will be worse at night, usually between midnight and 2:00 a.m.; they're better if they're warm, they're better with warm drinks, and they're better sitting upright. They are chilled; in their feelings, they're restless and anxious. So think of burning pain and better warm, which is a keynote for Arsenicosum.

Bryonia—It is a remedy for a dry, painful cough. They will hold their chest when they cough. They are worse with the slightest motion. A deep cough will make them worse. They're worse if they're lying. If they have sputum, they will have blood streak, sticky or hard sputum usually. So think of Bryonia when it becomes worse with slightest motion, so they'll hold their chest or their throat when they cough; wherever the cough's coming from the person needing, Bryonia will try to support or splint the area.

Causticum—Folks with a Causticum cough will have a marked tickling; it's very irritated. And actually, Causticum people are very irritating. They'll have a cough often with a wheeze. They are very intensely emotional people. They are better in the damp or rainy weather, which is a bit odd for most folks. Most folks are a bit worse at that time. Think of Causticum if there is an irritated, tickling cough, or a cough in the chest that's irritating. With a Causticum cough, they are often better once they've coughed something out.

Cuprum—They will have paroxysms of coughing and spasmodic-sounding cough. They may have cramping in their feet or hands with the cough. And the other funny thing about cuprum is, if they have cramps in their hands and feet, in their feet, the big toe will go up toward the sky, whereas usually if you have a cramp in your foot, you curl your foot toward the sole. That big toe's cramp-up position is a keynote for Cuprum. So if cramping, think Cuprum. The cough is going to be cramping or spasmodic. These folks will be better with cold drinks. They'll want to drink something cold to stop their cough. Their expectorant or sputum will be tough, blood-streaked, with a metallic taste. With metallic taste, think metal, Cuprum is a metal, so that might be of help in remembering Cuprum.

Drosera—They will have violent paroxysms of choking cough. They will have difficulty catching their breath, so they're going to look blue even. They're worse after midnight or first lying down. They have a retching cough, almost like they're going to vomit. They can have bloody nose with cough. They're better sitting or walking slowly.

More Remedies for Coughs

Antimonium Tartricum—There is a loud rattling, exhaustive cough. They're almost too weak to expel what's in their lungs. They're better if they're able to cough up the thick mucus. It's a little like Causticum, but it's more exhaustive, and they're weak sounding while Causticum is very irritating.

Hepar Sulphuricum—This is a dry or productive cough with a thick yellow mucus. They have pain, and they'll be hoarse, and they're worse with the slightest draft. They're worse uncovering, which would create a draft, and are better warm. Sulphur also tends to be yellow, and so if there's any yellow color, think of Sulphur. Hepar Sulphuricum tends to have a lot of mucus or pus to it—pretty ugly looking.

Ipecac—They will have, again, paroxysms of dry, irritative cough with frequent vomiting, and you know syrup of Ipecac creates vomiting. They're worse at night, usually at 7:00 p.m. or first hour in the morning. They're worse when eating or in a warm room. They're better if they have a cold drink or after they get something coughed out.

Pulsatilla—They have a cough that is dry at night and juicy in the morning. It's a juicy green cough. They'll have juicy green snot often. They're worse if they're warm or lying down. In the nighttime, they're worse if they're warm. They're better if there's open air and if they did gentle walking. This is the windflower; they like a slight breeze and are so different from the draft-hating Sulphur.

Sulphur—They have a lingering or neglected cough. They're worse at 11:00 a.m. or at night; the cough will disturb their sleep. Sulphur is a good remedy if you're not sure what else to give, or if the person is sick and tired of being sick.

Coccus Cacti—This person will cough up ropes of thick mucus. It's usually most prominent from 6:00 to 7:00 am, and also, Coccus Cacti will have a paroxysmal tickling cough. They're better in the cold and open air or with cold drinks and cold foods. So think Coccus Cacti and the ropy mucus produced with the cough.

Influenza

Influenza is defined as a dry, sometimes moist, cough; it is characterized by high fever, often greater than 100 degrees, sore throat, and muscle aches. Usually, it is a respiratory illness although a few people do have some gastrointestinal complaints, like vomiting or diarrhea, but those folks are rarely positive for influenza.

When you're exposed to influenza, or someone with the flu coughs in your face, consider the following:

Oscillococcinum—This is a Boiron product. Take 2-3 doses, 4-8 hours apart as needed. The instructions on the packet are to take an entire vial. It comes in 3, 6, and larger vial packets. More practically, you can pour a third of the vial into a quarter to a half cup of distilled or filtered water and let it dissolve, stir 10 times with a metal spoon, and take 1 teaspoon every 4-8 hours. Please keep the glass and the plussed dose in a dark space. You may also treat others with the same dilution. So with the quarter to a half cup, a quarter cup, you probably can get 12 or more doses out of that small amount. This solution should be remade daily if still needed. For prevention, when exposed, usually only 3 doses are needed. If you are exposed, you will not have symptoms, and by taking the remedy right away, this should prevent illness and often does.

Influenzinum—This is a 30C concentration, and again, you take 2-3 doses, which is 1 to 3 pellets, 4-8 hours apart. You may obtain Influenzinum from Helios Pharmaceuticals online. This is the nosode of influenza virus. Again, when used as a preventative measure when one has a known exposure, one need usually take 3 doses.

Influenza Prevention

Influenzinum—Take 30C once a month with additional doses if exposed as previously discussed above.

Influenza Vaccine Remedy—It's made from that year's flu vaccine remedy. So for 2010, it would say Influenza Vaccine Remedy 2010/2011. It may be obtained at Helios, and you take 30C once monthly. This is a good alternative, either of these, if you are sensitive to the influenza vaccine or its components or are unable, for any other reason because of reactions, to take the allopathic vaccine but must be immunized.

Influenza Treatment

First Sign of Illness: There are three remedies to choose if you have symptoms of influenza with chills, fever, dry cough, aching.

You can use **Oscillococcinum** at the first sign of any symptoms, and it's 2-3 doses, 4-8 hours apart. See the directions above for plussing the Oscillococcinum. If you're better, then stop.
If not better, consider these other two remedies:

Aconite—This is to be taken after a cold dry wind or chill. So take at the first sneeze or fever when there is no clear picture of the symptom, just the exposure. Take 30C or 3 doses, one every hour or so. If this works and you're feeling better, stop. If that doesn't work, the next remedy is as follows:

Ferrum Phosphoricum—This is what you'll want to take if Aconite doesn't help. Take 30C or 3 doses, one every hour, 1 to 3 pellets. Both of these remedies, Aconite and Ferrum Phosphoricum, are 30C in concentration.

Influenza—Symptomatic Treatment

The following remedies will be by symptomatic treatment, and this is, perhaps, after you've tried the other remedies mentioned—Aconite and Ferrum Phosphoricum and Oscillococcinum—and you still have symptoms.

Arsenicum Album—30C. The symptoms of flu are great prostration, and they are chilly, irritable, anxious, and quite fussy. They will have nasal and eye discharge that is watery and acrid or burning. They will have fevers with extreme chilliness. They will be thirsty for warm drinks. Everything will be better from heat. Remember that with Arsenicosum, we talked about cough, a burning sensation, that is better with heat, the same thing here, They are again very chilly. The one exception in the influenza with Arsenicum Album is that the headache will be worse from heat and better with fresh air. So they'll probably have everything covered except their head (Arsenicosum is also called Arsenicum Album).

Baptisia— 30C. This influenza has a terribly sudden onset. The person will feel sore and bruised all over; the limbs will feel like they're scattered and in bits. It's quite uncomfortable. They will have profuse sweat with a high fever and intense thirst. Their faces will appear as dull and red, and they almost look stuporous. They will be dazed, and this is an excellent remedy for gastric flu with vomiting and diarrhea. So think of Baptisia if the symptoms are as described above.

Bryonia Alba—This is a flu that will come on slowly, and they will ache all over especially in the joints. Again, as characterized with Bryonia symptoms, they will be worse from least movement. They will be very irritable and want to be left alone. This person will be quite upset if you jar the bed even or sit down beside them and move the bed; they will feel worse. They will be very thirsty, but it will be painful for them to drink because it hurts to swallow. They will have a dry, painful cough and will have a headache from the cough.

Eupatorium Perfoliatum—This is a remedy where pain is felt as if the bones are broken. This patient will moan and groan in pain. Even their eyeballs will hurt. They will have a bursting headache; they will crave ice-cold water, which brings on a violent chill that will start in the low back. They will have very little sweat, but if they sweat, they will be better from sweat. So consider Eupatorium if there's a broken bone sensation and if there's moaning and groaning and they're thirsty for cold water even though they get a chill from that.

Gelsemium—Gelsemium happens when the weather changes from cold to warm. This is a flu that is pretty common in Minnesota, where we have a frequent change in weather. It'll come on slowly; they'll feel very weak, and they'll have aching muscles that feel heavy. They'll have a dull headache, and they're thirstless even with a fever, which is a bit unusual. They will have chills that go up and down their spine. They're apathetic and drowsy. Gelsemium is a remedy of extreme weakness, so think of that remedy if you have a weak sensation with influenza.

Mercurius Solubilis—The people who need Mercurius Solubilis will have a fever with a copious (large amount) offensive sweat. They will be worse from sweat. They will also have bad breath, and they may have a dark and dirty tongue. They will have increased salivation and will be very thirsty. Perhaps you're aware of mercury poisoning, where you tend to get drooling and have a dirty-looking tongue which will be a characteristic of Mercurius influenza.

Nux Vomica—The Nux remedy will have a gastric influenza with a lot of vomiting and diarrhea along with aching limbs and back. Their nose will run in the day and will be dry at night. They will have fever and chills, which is worse when drinking. They are so chilled it's hard for those who need Nux Vomica to get warm. And they are sensitive to the least draft, even a slight uncovering of their bed covers. They will be very irritable and impatient as patients, so this will be the picture of Nux Vomica influenza.

Pyrogenium—In a patient with a very serious flu, you'd need Pyrogenium. It's a flu with severe back and limb pain. They will have a terrible bursting headache. They will feel beaten and bruised all over, and even the bed feels hard so they are unable to rest well. They will have chills on both their back and their limbs with a thumping heart. They are very restless; they're better on the start of movement, but they cannot find a comfortable position. Actually, in patients who need Pyrogenium, you need to watch them carefully because these are some of the people that may need to be transferred to the hospital for further hospital and allopathic support, such as oxygen, IV fluids, other cares and comfort. But try Pyrogenium. If it doesn't work, consider transferring them as soon as possible.

Rhus Toxicodendron—This flu will start in the cold damp weather. There's an aching with stiffness. They're worse with first movement, actually better with movement, but they get so easily tired. So they're quite restless. They hurt when they're still. They try to move, and they feel a little better, but then they're worse. They are better from warmth, usually a dry heat. They're quite anxious and weepy in characteristics. If you consider Rhus Toxicodendron, which is poison oak, it's a restless rash—better if you scratch it—and it's a weepy rash, and these characteristics might help you better remember this remedy for the flu.

Dosing for Influenza

The dose is 30C or anything available if someone is more severely ill. You usually can take it every 1-4 hours, 1-2 if they're more severely ill, and less often (every 3-4 hours) if they're not so bad. Take as needed for the symptoms. If they're better, stop. Restart if symptoms return. If you take 6 doses and there is absolutely no change and no improvement, then consider reviewing the symptoms to look for a different remedy. If, again, a person is on a constitutional remedy, please check with their homeopath because that may treat the symptoms that they're having or there may be a specific remedy that may work best for them.

Sore Throat / Pharyngitis

Aconite—Again, this remedy will work well for a sore throat where it's dry, red, and burning and if it suddenly appears after a cold wind or a chill. It's the very characteristic for any Aconite illness. They will have a fever; they'll be anxious and fearful. They might even have the appearance of a deer in the headlight because they're so anxious. So consider Aconite especially when illness occurs after a cold dry wind or a significant chill.

Belladonna—Belladonna is for acute tonsillitis. It will be rapidly appearing; it will usually be a right-sided tonsillitis with burning pain. They will be worse with the slightest touch, worse when turning their head. Their tongue will appear red and strawberry looking.

Lachesis—For Lachesis, the tonsils will be a deep red and purple in color. They often start on the left and move to the right side. They are worse when swallowing, especially liquids. As a keynote, these folks are better if they swallow solids. They'll also feel like they'll have a lump or constricted sensation in the throat. Left—to right-sided sore throat and better swallowing of food are keynote characteristics for Lachesis.

Hepar Sulphuricum—The person with the Hepar sore throat will have suppurative tonsils or pharynx; this means lots of pus, and they'll look quite nasty. The sensation in the throat will be like fish bone or that a splinter is poking in a Hepar sore throat. They will be worse with cold air, worse with cold drink, worse with cold food. They will be much better from warmth or warm drink. So consider Hepar with suppurative tonsils or a lot of discharge or, as we say in medicine, exudate.

Lycopodium—Lycopodium is worse from four to eight in the evening; it is right sided in the tonsils and goes to the left side and is much better with warm or cold drink. It's the opposite of Lachesis, which is better with food and goes left to right. Lycopodium goes right to the left and is better with warm or cold drink and worse with food.

Apis—The Apis sore throat is burning and with stinging pain and with a great deal of swelling and redness. They are better with cold food or drink. Apis is the honeybee, and if you recall from being stung, usually there is a lot of redness and burning and stinging pain. So consider that, and that might help you remember the Apis sore throat.

Argentum Nitricum—Those needing Argentum Nitricum will have a stitching or splinter-like pain in the throat; they will also lose their voice, which is usually from overuse through performance or speaking. Laryngitis or hoarseness is very common in this type of sore throat. There is much clearing of the throat in Argentum Nitricum sore throat.

Baryta Carbonica—The tonsils are hugely swollen. There are large and hard cervical glands in the neck. They are worse at night. They are worse when speaking. They have marked pain on empty swallowing as well as on clearing the throat. Baryta Carbonica is often associated with the mono tonsillitis where you have both the swollen cervical neck glands and the hugely swollen tonsils. Baryta would be a great remedy for that particular tonsillitis/laryngitis.

Bryonia—Bryonia will have a dry throat and mouth. They will have a very increased thirst. They will be worse with any motion, like swallowing, speaking, or coughing. So in a Bryonia sore throat, you'll often see them holding or grasping at their throat or neck as they swallow to help decrease the movement. And remember, Bryonia is the remedy that is worse with least motion. So this would be quite an uncomfortable sore throat.

Mercurius Vivus—As with the previously discussed mercury, there's bad breath, there's drooling, and there's a dirty tongue. These folks will be worse at night, worse with the heat of the bed, and worse with the least change of temperature to hot or cold. As you know, mercury is what we used to measure temperature in the past, not so much now, and it is very sensitive to temperature change. Hence, think Mercurius Vivus if there's a sensitivity to change in temperature, they have bad breath, they're drooling, and they have a dirty tongue.

Silica—Silica is an excellent remedy for a recurring sore throat or for a peritonsillar abscess, or there is a feeling that there is a hair in the back of the tongue. With Silica, there are enlarged and hard cervical neck glands. Silica folks tend to be generally cold, and they are worse when they become cold. So think of Silica for the recurring sore throat or the peritonsillar abscess. Silica's a great remedy for abscesses in general.

Dosing for a sore throat—Take 30C of a specific remedy, or if they're on a constitutional, that might work for their sore throat. You want to give the 30C at least 3 times a day or every 3-4 hours for 3-4 doses. If they aren't changing or they're getting worse, you need to seek allopathic care or further assistance. If they're better, stop the remedy. If symptoms recur, you may restart. Again, it is important to pay attention to the symptoms of the patient.

Earaches: Otitis Media

Definition: *Otitis media* is the infection of the middle ear, redness of the eardrum, or fluid behind the eardrum; *otitis externa* is an infection of the ear canal and also called swimmer's ear. Internal ear infections usually result in dizziness and are not necessarily covered in this chapter. Inner ear infections are called *labrynthitis*, which has dizziness and tinnitus or *vestibular neuronitis*, which has dizziness that lasts less than 6 weeks. If tinnitus (ringing in the ears) and dizziness last longer than 6 weeks, this may be a sign of Ménière's disease. *Ménière's disease* can lead to hearing loss as can severe middle or inner ear infections. With inner ear infections, there is rarely pain involved. Otitis media is the most common cause of ear pain or earaches. Otitis externa is less common but frequent cause of ear pain, especially if wiggling the earlobe or pinna causes pain.

Acute earaches may be treated with Chamomilla, Belladonna, Ferrum Phosphoricum, Hepar Sulph, Mercurius, and Pulsatilla.

Chronic earaches—Pulsatilla, Mercurius, Silica, Calcarea Carbonica, Lycopodium, Medorrhinum, Sulphur, and Tuberculinum.

Right-sided earaches—Mercurius, Mercurious Iodatus Flavus, Belladonna, Lycopodium, and Nitric Acid.

Left-sided earaches—Mercurious Iodatus Ruber, Sulphur, Lachesis, Medorrhinum, Kali Bichromicum

Otitis

Chamomilla—This will have exquisitely painful earaches; they're worse when touching the ear. They're better if they're carried. This is the screaming, demanding child who wishes to be carried and then put down. There will be no pus in Chamomilla. They're quite irritable in disposition.

Mercurius—This person will have a history of many infections. There is a yellow-green offensive discharge. They're worse at night, worse with damp, worse with the heat of the bed, sensitive to temperature change as mercury is.

Pulsatilla—All upper respiratory infections (URI) lead to ear infections. This is a painful, bursting sensation in the ear. It's usually left sided. It's worse in the heat. It's better in the open cool air and better being carried with a gentle motion. Pulsatilla is a windflower so they like a wee bit of a breeze.

Silica—Silica is the main remedy for chronic serous otitis in which there is fluid in the ear that never clears. Persistant fluid may lead to hearing loss and chronic pain. It's the first remedy for hearing loss from otitis media. Silica folks are worse with cold and uncovering; they're worse with wind and loud noises. It's a quiet, fragile-looking child. Often they'll have light-colored skin, blond, thin, fragile-looking, light skin—a porcelain look to the skin.

Aconite—As you can guess, Aconite will be an earache that appears after a sudden onset after a chill or cold wind. It will often be left ear; there often is a high fever, flushed face, and a great deal of thirst. And they might be quite fearful or anxious-fearful in their look.

Belladonna—There is a sudden onset of a pulsating, unbearable ear pain. There is a terrible throbbing pain especially on the right side. It's worse at 3:00 pm; it's worse with any jarring. It's associated with a flushed red face; there's high fever, dilated pupils, and the hands and feet will be cold even though the face is red and flushed looking.

Calcarea Carbonica—Every cold leads to ear infection like Pulsatilla, but these folks are worse in the cold weather or if there is a change of weather. They are kind of a thick-looking person; they have the pudgy-baby look to them. A sturdy child is what one would say when you think of Calcarea Carbonica.

Ferrum Phosporicum—This is an acute otitis media (OM) with sudden onset of severe pain and high fever. It is often right sided; they will want consolation and comfort.

Hepar Sulphur—This person will have an acute onset in a very sensitive child. They'll wake up screaming with pain. They'll hate to be examined or touched; they're going to be worse late at night, and they're worse in cold or open air. They're better if they wrap their ear so they'll come in with the hat on their head or their hand covering their ear to keep it warm. That's a Hepar Sulphur. They might have some pus as one might expect with Hepar infections.

Lachesis—It is a severe left-side pain, sometimes with a dark bloody discharge; they're worse at night, worse in heat, worse when swallowing. They're better when lying on the left side, better if they're boring their finger in the ear, better with cold air, or better when sitting up. As a way to remember Lach, which is a snake that eats solid food and swallow whole, remember sore throat—better when swallowing solids and the finger to the ear canal is a lot like swallowing something whole in the throat. Similar comfort is brought to the person with a Lachesis earache.

Lycopodium—It is right sided, where the earache begins on the right and goes to the left. It's worse in the afternoon, 4:00-8:00 p.m. It's worse in cold or open air; and worse with warm applications. They will crave sweets and warm drinks. They're anxious, and they'll desire company nearby. So think of Lycopodium in the afternoon about tea time, and it is right sided.

Nitric Acid—There is chronic pain and inflammation, stitching, poking pains. It's worse at night, worse when swallowing, worse when cold, and much better when warm.

Kali Muriaticum—One will have a chronic glue ear-crackling or popping feeling when swallowing or jaw movement. This is the ear infection that has fluid remaining that does not clear. It's not necessarily painful whereas Silica would be painful.

Dosage for otitis media—It depends on the severity. Usually, 30C every 3-6 hours or every 4 hours for a couple of days. They should be looking better after 4 doses.

Over-the-counter medication: Similasan Earache Relief Ear Drops—This is a generic homeopathic earache treatment. There is a children's formulation, and I'd suggest purchasing that because adults can use children's. This contains the following:

Chamomilla (10X)
Mercurius Solubilis (15X)
Sulphur (12 X)
Pulsatilla* (12X) (*The latter is in the children's only.)

You can get this at Fresh & Natural Foods, Walgreens, Target, and CVS. This is a good generic medication that may be used. It affects healing in 85 percent of infections which is equal to antibiotics. As you know, it does not cover all the infections, and we have a few more remedies to choose from. But it's a nice choice to try and may be used if there is no drainage out the ear. *Any drainage, do not put these eardrops in.* It has *not* been tested with ruptured eardrums. That's another consideration. Similasan is an excellent choice to have in your medicine cabinet as a go-to drop. Similasan also works for external otitis or swimmer's ear.

Mucous Production

Muriates—tend to have egg white-colored mucus

Carbonates—tend to be clear to yellow

Sulfates—yellow mucus, as we talked about earlier

Sycotic remedies—tend to be green, as we mentioned those different remedies, Medorrhinum, for example, just as a summary here

Urinary Tract Infections

May include the bladder, kidneys, urethra because it's based on symptomatology. With signs of kidney infections—back pain and fever—one suggests antibiotics, both allopathic and homeopathic treatments, as destruction of the kidneys is a significant physiologic event, and one doesn't want to have that as a complication.

Cantharis—There is an intense burning, scalding acid pain before, during, and after urination. It's better with cold applications after the bladder is empty. It's worse with drinking. Think of *pain* for urinary tract infection, then consider Cantharis.

Nux Vomica—There will be constant urging and a full sensation in the bladder, but only small amounts of urine will be excreted on urination. For *frequent urging*, think Nux Vomica.

Pulsatilla—There is sudden urgency, and pain is worse if urge is postponed. There is burning feeling during and after urination. They feel worse lying down on back, worse in cold wet weather. *Pain—irregular paroxysmal, spurting.*

Sarsaparilla—This person will have copious (lots of) urination, burning pain just at the end, the last few drops; usually there's blood at the last few drops. They're worse in the cold and damp. If there is *pain at the end of urination,* consider Sarsaparilla.

Apis—Apis has burning pain. They're better when cold and have scanty urine. Perhaps one way to remember this is Apis is the honeybee, and they don't drink much, and they don't urinate much. So think of little but burning as the sting. *Scanty urine, better cold,* consider Apis.

Aconite—The symptoms appear after cold, chill, or fright exposure; there is urine retention in a newborn or in a woman after labor and delivery, which is a significant cold or fright exposure for both mom and the newborn often. *Cold chill or fright, retention of newborn or mother post delivery*—Aconite.

Staphysagria—There will be burning and bladder spasm during and long after completion of urination. It's also UTI after sexual activity or coition. *Honeymoon cystitis, after coition*—Staphysagria.

Dosage for urinary tract infections: Usually 30C every 2 hours until the symptoms subside. If there's no improvement after 3 doses, retake the case and look at the symptoms. If they're on a constitutional remedy, which also covers urinary tract infections, that would be a better choice as a 12C or 30C, but check with their homeopath.
Seek medical help if symptoms are worse or back pain and/or fever develops.

Summary

We have discussed several common acute illnesses at home:

> coughs
> influenza
> sore throat
> earaches
> UTIs

Treatment with specific acute remedy or if on a constitutional remedy, consult their homeopath.
If there is not a reasonable response or if symptoms are worse, one needs to be evaluated by the allopathic system in urgent care or primary care provider or emergency room until symptoms decrease.

Review Quiz

1. Which remedy do you think of for cough, flu, sore throat, earache that happens after a chill or cold dry wind?
2. Which remedy has burning pain, discharges, makes the person feels chilled, and is better warm? It's used for cough, flu, and sore throat.
3. Which remedy has burning pain with scanty urine and is better with cold?

4. Which remedy has a dry cough, dry throat, very thirsty? They're worse with least movement. It's for a cough, flu, cold, or sore throat.

5. Which remedy starts from left to right, is better with solids, worse with liquids, is worse lying on the left, is better in cool open air, and is better sitting up? It's for sore throat or otitis media.

6. Every cold leads to an earache. Which two remedies fall under that category?

7. Now here's a list for UTI remedies. Which is the most common symptom?

    A. Pain?
    B. Frequent urination?
    C. Pain at end of urination with copious urine?
    D. UTI after coition?
    E. Urine scanty?
    F. Retention in newborn or woman after labor?

(Answers are on page 75.)

Homeopathy for First Aid—Part I

(If included, please insert disk 3: Homeopathy for First Aid—Part I)

We will review the following:

- Homeopathic guide rules
- First aid rules
- Stroke
- Sunstroke
- Shock, collapse, and lightning
- Bites and stings
- Allergic reactions
- Appendicitis
- Food poisoning

Homeopathic Guide Rules

- Symptoms matter—like treats like.
- A little goes a long way because this is energy medicine.
- Dosing frequency depends upon the severity and the vital force strength.
- Plussing—method of dosing which allows for variation and increasing of the dose.
- Remember to follow first aid rules.
- Seek medical care when needed.
- If a person is on a constitutional remedy, consult their homeopath.

First Aid Rules

- Assess the situation—*Think first, then act.*
- The *A, B, C,* and *D*s—Start with the most life-threatening issue first. *A* is airway, *B* is breathing, *C* is circulation, and *D* is dispatch 911.
- Call 911 and get help from others.
- First, use routine remedies, then rely on symptoms, getting down to two to three remedies.
- Consider formal first aid/CPR training by the American Red Cross or the American Heart Association.

Stroke

A stroke is either caused by a clot or a bleed into the brain tissue. The usual symptoms are confusion, abnormality in talking, one-sided weakness of face or body, loss of consciousness or coma. This may be associated with a very severe headache or head pain never felt before. It is important to bring anyone you feel is having a stroke to the emergency room for evaluation. If unconscious, use the first aid *A, B, C, D*s to support until further care can be obtained. Homeopathy may be used as indicated along with supportive and emergency care.

Minor Stroke

The first symptoms of a minor stroke are usually headache, dizziness, or confusion. Later, speech, memory, or partial paralysis may ensue.

Aconite—30C to be given at first sign if restless or anxious or fearful

Arnica—30C, 3 times a day for several days to promote blood absorption if stroke is known and it's minor

Get them to the hospital as soon as possible as a minor stroke may herald a major stroke.

Minor strokes used to be called TIAs, transient ischemic attacks, and now are considered preemptive strokes. So consider them as a full-blown stroke until proven otherwise over time.

Major Stroke

The symptoms of a major stroke are unconsciousness, with difficulty breathing, unequal pupils, and incontinence of bowel or bladder.

First Aid: Perform first aid first, do the *A, B, C, D*s—airway, breathing, circulation, and dial 911.

Arnica—Give it in the highest dose you have. Remember that Arnica covers both bleeding and bruising and clotting, so it's a great remedy for major stroke.

Opium—Give 30C every 5 minutes if the face is flushed and there's noisy breathing. Stop when the patient comes to. This is a patient who is unconscious that you would give opium to. It could be lifesaving.

There are very few remedies for strokes: **Aconite, Arnica,** and **Opium.** Use the one that fits the symptoms most.

With stroke, it is important to get emergency room care to help maintain and restore vital function of the brain. Now in allopathic care treatment, strokes may be treated with thrombolytic agents to dissolve clots and stents or other care, sometimes surgical care, to stop bleeding if needed.

Heart Attack

Heart attacks are actually strokes of the heart. They are either a clot or a bleeding in the heart vessels. The symptoms are often chest pain, left-arm pain, jaw pain, or pain that radiates to the left arm or jaw, sweating, vomiting, nausea, indigestion, pale skin, and shortness of breath. These are mostly male symptoms. Symptoms for females can vary with odd pains—not always on the left side or with sweating or nausea and not always radiating to the left arm or neck—but the pains are usually associated with movement or activity, improving or resolving at rest. Angina is a spasm of the vessels or less flow when more is needed by the heart to perform more strenuous activity, like exercise or digestion, after a large meal.

If a heart attack is even considered, treat for a heart attack.

Have the person *chew an aspirin*; it doesn't matter if it's an *81 mg or 325 mg. Call 911*. Take them by ambulance to the emergency room. It's very important to get someone to emergency care as soon as possible to prevent further loss of the function of the heart or function of the person.

Give remedies until help arrives or while transporting to the hospital.

First Remedies for Heart Attacks

Arnica—30C-200C to 1M given until symptoms improve. Remember, this is the remedy for acute shock to the system (in this case, the heart) where there is bleeding or clotting. Emotionally, this person will be stoic and continue doing what he is doing as if nothing is wrong.

Aconite—If the person thinks they'll die and/or are fearful, restless, consider Aconite. Aconite is more like shock—a shock of fear—and patients may have the look of the deer in the headlights.

Arsenicosum—It is another good remedy if they're very anxious and restless and know they are going to die and they are much more anxious than Aconite.

Latrodectus—It is for pain that radiates to the axilla (armpit).

Cactus—It is for constricting pain and for a fluttering sensation of the heart.

Dosing for suspected heart attack: Give the dose that you have (30C or if you have higher, you may give 200C especially if they have a really strong emotional component).

Sunstroke

Sunstroke is life threatening. The person is unconscious with a rapid pulse, and the body temperature is usually greater than 105 and 106. With sunstroke, there may be no perspiration at all.

Heatstroke is less severe and a bit more common. The heatstroke patient is awake and is sweating. It's not as life threatening but can lead to sunstroke if care is not taken.

The *treatment for sunstroke is to immediately cool the body*—ice on the four corners: the axilla and the groin creases, and to the head. Make sure there's a cloth barrier so you don't create frostbite in these areas. They need to have good fluids, orally if conscious, or IV, intravenously, if not conscious, and make sure there's support for circulation and breathing. Rather obviously is that 911 should be called if unconscious and cannot be roused.

Remedies

Glonium—This is the treatment of choice at 30C. Give Glonium as soon as the temperature is decreasing. If the temperature is rising, wait for remedy use and apply cooling topically.

If not regaining consciousness, then compare Glonium, which has a flushed face, is unconscious but with an acute, rapid pulse; **Belladonna**—they're going to have a flushed face with dilated eyes; or **Nat Carb**—they're pretty stuporous and not able to answer. You can also give all three; alternate one and then repeat the next in 5 minutes and so on. So every 5 minutes, you can give a different remedy. As soon as they respond, stop, and of course, get support for them as soon as possible.

Shock or Collapse

Shock or collapse is potentially fatal, especially if not treated. They will have pale, clammy skin that will feel cold; there's weakness over all, a rapid, thready pulse, and irregular breathing. This is preceding circulatory collapse, which is fatal if that occurs and there is no intravenous support of fluids or blood.

First aid—Have them lie down if they are not already. Elevate their feet. Stop any bleeding. Use the *A, B, C,* and *D.* Call 911.

Remedies

Aconite—To be given if they're anxious, fearful, and if Arnica doesn't work.

Arnica is the mainstay if there's injury or they're having shock or collapse and especially if they say, "I am okay," and they're in shock. The dose would be 30C-200C.

Carbo Vegetabilis—These folks will be torpid and sluggish. They'll feel cold, they'll crave fresh air, and they'll even have a cold breath. There may be signs of asphyxiation, which would be treated well with Carbo Veg. They certainly will be quite depleted and, again, rather at end stage. This is a time for 911. So this is an important remedy to actually give on the way to the emergency room.

Veratrum Album—Here, the folks will appear blue, cold, with cold sweat on the forehead. They'll feel freezing cold, thirsty. So a little bit different from Carbo Veg (where they would be more sluggish and nonresponsive). Here, they'll be blue with cold sweat, but their breath will not be cold, but they will be weak.

Other Shock Remedies

Bach's RESCUE Remedy—This is for *emotional shock, fear, shock, panic, trembling, fainting, acute pain;* it can be used in any emergency. Drops are placed on the tongue and repeated as needed. It's of flower essences, and Bach was a student of Hahnemann.

Ignatia—Ignatia is an excellent remedy to use if it's an *emotional shock or disbelief, grief, hysteria,* recent loss like somebody was killed in the war and this person finds out and goes into shock. Ignatia is the perfect remedy for that.

Phosphorus—Phosphorus is for an *acute lightning strike* or the *ill effects of an electric shock* that puts someone into shock. Consider Phosphorus.

Morphinum—It is used for *lightning strike if Phosphorus does not work* or is not sufficient.

Dosing in shock: In all cases, 30C can be given every 15 minutes until improvement occurs.

Bites and Stings

In homeopathy, it does not matter the source of the bite or sting, whether snake, insect, mosquito, bee, or jellyfish, etc. All are treated by the symptoms expressed, and the severity of the reaction may dictate a need for EpiPen or ER visit or visit to allopath if infection or poisoning occurs.

Simple Stings

This is a local reaction. Usually, a dose of 30C every 15 minutes until improved and then 4 times a day until all symptoms are resolved. This is the normal dosing for a simple sting.

Topical treatments

    Urtica Urens—prickly reaction

Hypericum tinctures—nerve pain or shooting pain from the site
Ledum tinctures—puncture sting and cool local reaction

Tinctures are these plants dissolved in alcohol, and this is more of an herbal treatment, but they work well for mild reactions as noted above.

Ledum Palustre is the first for minor symptoms where the area feels cold and numb, and it is also better with cold. So cold, better cold with numbness, think of Ledum. Ledum will cover any puncture wound with these symptoms.

Apis Mellifica—There will be great swelling, redness with burning and stinging, and is better from cold. Think the usual reaction to bee sting—that's Apis.

Cantharis—The site is red and angry with burning, and if you recall, Cantharis was the most painful of all the urinary treatment remedies for pain and burning. So that's Cantharis. Cantharis is more painful but has less swelling than Apis.

Tarentula Cubensis—The part that is injured is blue. There is burning at the area of the blue color.

Lachesis—It is for bites with lymphadenitis. Lymphadenitis is the red streak that goes up the arm, sometimes called blood poisoning, although that's not what it is since it's inflammation of the lymphatic system. So consider Lachesis for a red line extending from the bite site.

Anaphylaxis

Anaphylaxis is life threatening. You need to be prepared to perform CPR. If you have an EpiPen, use it and call 911. While waiting for emergency help, choose and give an appropriate remedy from the following:

Carbolic Acid—Give 30C every 5 minutes until there's improvement. It's especially good if there's a bee sting. If you don't have Carbolic Acid, then use Apis Mellifica, which should be used if carbolic acid is not working.

Anaphylaxis is the swelling and thickening of the tongue and airways. Because of the marked swelling, there is the risk of losing the ability to breathe if the airway swells enough to close. So it is a 911 emergency. So you need to do all you can with these two remedies—use any dose that you have, call 911, and get supportive care. If you have an EpiPen, just give it. Our goal is to not risk their life.

Venomous Bites and Stings

This is different from just a sting or a bite because venomous means that it's systemic or septic, an effect which is different because usually a bite or sting is local. But if there is a systemic reaction, anaphylaxis could be one reaction, which we'd treat as previously discussed. Venom is another, and remedies or specific antidotes are another form of treatment.

First Aid—Remove the stinger or tentacles; use a constricting band or anything to support the injured limb so it doesn't go further. To remove a stinger, a good way is to use a piece of tape and pull it out as opposed to using tweezers so you don't squeeze more of the venom into the person.

Remedies

Apis—There is much swelling, redness, stinging pain, and it is better cold as we've discussed.

Ledum—The affected part is cold, numb, and it feels better cold.

Hypericum—The pain is so severe, and it shoots out from the wound. The pain is worse than it appears, so you don't see the injury much, but there's a lot of pain. Think Hypericum, which affects the nervous system preferentially.

Lachesis—It's often on the left side; lymphadenitis is that blood-poisoning look, so think Lachesis.

Cantharis—If there's a hot, burning red wound with much pain, think Cantharis. Cantharis has less swelling than Apis.

Allergic Reactions

Hives and food allergies—This is as an acute reaction of a rash or swelling of the skin. There may be swelling of the lips called angioneurotic edema. More severe, anaphylaxis is general overall swelling that affects the mouth, oral mucosa, tongue, or airways, along with external rash, which is a medical emergency.

There are *three main remedies for allergic reaction*, with many smaller ones to consider. Allopathically, these would be treated with the antihistamines, the most commonly known is Benadryl (diphenhydramine) or steroids; either can be topical or oral in use. If there is systemic reaction, then epinephrine (EpiPen) and systemic support from emergency services are advised.

Urtica Urens—These are simple hives that burn and sting—kind of prickly or may be painless. There may be swelling under the skin like angioneurotic edema, where you get swelling of the lips. Urtica works well for this prickly rash. If there is more rash, less swelling. If it's worse with heat and bathing and better lying down and better with rubbing, then consider Urtica Urens.

Rhus Toxicodendron—These are very large red urticarial (itching) rash with prickling itching. They're worse cold, wet, if rubbed, or with fever. They're better with sweats or scalding water or dry heat. Choose Rhus Tox for this type of rash and allergic reaction.

Apis Mellifica—It has a reaction similar to Urtica, but it's more severe. There's more swelling; it's worse in heat and it's better with cold and can be used in anaphylaxis. There is much itching with Apis.

Histamine—Use this if Apis fails. There is redness and burning, and it feels better from fanning and direct pressure and worse with heat and irritation.

Carbolic Acid—This is best used in anaphylactic shock when the person is near collapse or is comatose. There's a dusky face, much swelling. It's another backup for Apis. One can give remedies to the unconscious by placing them inside the lip or in the mouth. The small pellets will not occlude an airway or cause choking!

Just as an aside—For known poison ivy or poison oak rash, dry it out with a hair dryer. Remember, Rhus tox (poison oak) is better in dry heat, and seal it with fresh aloe vera sap, which might improve the symptoms or decrease the discomfort.

Appendicitis

This is an acute condition. There is belly pain, usually in the right lower quadrant of the abdomen. There is often fever, along with anorexia or lack of appetite, and rebound tenderness—when you push on the area, it hurts, but when you let go, it hurts more. This can be life threatening, so you want to treat it right away and probably get them into the allopathic provider/emergency room as soon as possible. You will find that someone with appendicitis will often feel worse as they're moving or walking. The jarring of walking makes it worse.

The remedy of choice is **Bryonia**—30C every 15 minutes on the way to the emergency room. If you recall, Bryonia is worse with least movement, and it's the typical symptom of appendicitis. Surgery is the allopathic treatment of choice.

Food Poisoning

With many poisons, you need to follow first aid treatment to reduce exposure, dilute, or expel the toxin.

Call Poison Control—1-800-222-1212. If you have the bottle of what's taken and the ingredients, they can give you specific instructions on what to do. They are most helpful at Poison Control.
If the patient has been treated but still has symptoms, it is then time to consider homeopathy.

Arsenicum Album—There is great exhaustion, and they are anxious, restless; there is severe vomiting and purging—vomiting and diarrhea (from either end). They can be very chilly or hot; there's a putrid smell to them. Emotionally, they are anxious and restless as are most folks who benefit from Arsenicosum.

Veratrum Album—It is like above with vomiting and diarrhea, but they have a cold sweat, cold breath, and blueness. The extremities feel cold as death, and vomiting and purging are often happening simultaneously—from both ends at the same time. That's Veratrum with that blue color as we've previously discussed. These folks may need fluid assistance to restore the loss from purging.

Carbo Vegetabilis—They have cold, collapsed appearance. They crave fresh air even though they're cold. Again, this is a near-shock condition, so consider transfer to medical care obviously if not responsive.

Cuprum Metallicum—Their cramps are outrageous. They have abdominal cramps from the food poisoning or may have other muscle cramps from the poisoning as they're sick. Think Cuprum for cramps.

Treatment dosage for food poisoning: Give 30C with each episode of vomit or stool. Stop when they are better. If 3-4 doses are given and there's no change, reconsider the remedy choice. Reevaluate symptoms: if they're getting worse or are near collapse, then the emergency room is needed for supportive measures. They may need to be hospitalized for IV fluids, rehydration, and medication to slow down their symptoms. However, the body does better by getting the poison out, which it's trying to do by vomiting and purging.

Review Quiz

1. In first aid, what do *A, B, C, D* mean?
2. Homeopathy takes the place of allopathic treatment. True or false?
3. An allergic reaction with red, hot, much swelling, worse in heat, better in cold would suggest the need for which remedy?
4. Appendicitis, pleuritic chest pain with cough, worse with least movement, which remedy would you consider using it?
5. Acute injury remedies:

   A. "Everything is fine," says the patient, who may have bruising and bleeding
   B. Anxious patients who know they will die and are anxious and very restless
   C. Fearful person, staring in shock, anxious in acute injury

(Answers are on page 76.)

Homeopathy for First Aid—Part II

(If included, please insert disc 4: Homeopathy for First Aid—Part II.)

We will cover the following areas in this section:
- Review of homeopathy and first aid
- Eye injuries
- Burns and frostbite
- Open wounds
- Contusions, bruises, and concussions
- Sprains and strains
- Bone fractures
- Surgeries

Homeopathic Guide Rules

- Symptoms matter—like treats like.
- A little goes a long way. It's energy medicine.
- Dosing frequency depends upon the severity and the strength of the vital force.
- Plussing allows variation of the dose and increasing of the dose each time as you add more strength energetically.
- Follow the first aid rules.
- Seek medical care when needed.
- If on a constitutional remedy, consult your homeopath.

First Aid Rules

- Assess the situation—*think first, then act.*
- The *A, B, C, D*s—start with the most life-threatening issue.
- *D*, of course, is call 911 dispatch and get help from others.

- First, use routine remedies. Then rely on symptoms, getting down to two to three remedies that best apply.
- Consider formal first aid/CPR training from the American Red Cross or the American Heart Association.

Eye Injuries

There are many types of eye injuries: blunt, sharp, foreign objects flying into the eye.

For any injury, consider **Arnica** or **Aconite** *to be given first*, depending on the patient's mood—Arnica if they're just fine, Aconite if they're really worried/fearful.

Hypericum—Give 30C every half hour if there's great pain. You can also dilute Hypericum tincture on a moist pad without getting it into the eye (since the tincture has alcohol) and place it over the closed eye. Sometimes, that will help with the pain. As you recall, Hypericum is about nerve pain, shooting pain, and often with eye injuries; a small wound causes a great deal of pain, so consider Hypericum for an eye injury.

First aid treatment for eyes: If the small object is present and removal is necessary, use first aid or rush to the emergency room.

If something is protruding from the globe, patch the good eye so they tend not to look around and further injure the other eye.

Also, to protect the bad eye, consider taping a cup over the eye so nothing hits or jars whatever is protruding.

If a large object is protruding out of the globe, don't pull it out, especially if it has punctured the globe. Protect it as discussed above and get more professional help.

If a liquid or small particles have flown into the eye rinse well with water. Do that as best you can. Go to the emergency room for a penetrating injury or a major injury.

Eye-Surface Irritations

Dilute with a decoction of Eyebright or Euphrasia. So you can just dilute it with Euphrasia, which is also Eyebright, and that will help.

Euphrasia—Give 30C if pain and discomfort persist, more for eye irritations like chemical to the eye after the chemical has been irrigated out.

Calendula—This is for a cut or scratched, abraded cornea, or cut cornea. If contact has been in too long, consider Calendula. Use Calendula 1M for eye surgery. If eye surgery is recently done and there is pain persisting, consider Calendula. This will help with the pain and encourage faster healing also.

Blunt Eye Injuries

An example of a blunt injury would be black eye, an injury that would not include a sharp instrument or cut to the eye. First aid treatment is usually cold pack or ice pack.

Ledum is the remedy preferred for black eye, better cold.
After using Ledum, consider the following:

Arnica if there are lots of bruising or bleeding in the eye.

Hypericum if there is shooting pain or mostly pain as the major complaint.

Symphytum is good for blunt injury to the eyeball but not necessarily the orbit or bones around the eye. If there is injury to the orbit with bruising, then Ledum preferred. Aching, pressing pain of the eye, consider Symphytum.

Dosage: Give 30C every 1 hour until better then reduce to dosing every 5 hours further decreasing as healing proceeds and when minimal symptoms reduce to twice a day until fully healed.

Sharp Eye Injuries

First aid treatment—immediate medical attention and to the emergency room.

Hypericum—This is if there's nerve pain. Hypericum is excellent for snow blindness. Sun reflected off snow at high altitudes where folks don't adequately cover or protect their eyes can actually lead to "sunburn" of the eyes. It is very painful.

Calendula—This is for all eye surgeries as previously mentioned.

Aconite—Consider this if there's extreme fright with an eye injury.

Calcarea—Consider this if the pain and weakness persist even though the injury is now healed and the eye is now recovered. Calcarea would be excellent for these persistent symptoms.

Burns

There are three descriptions of burns.

The older description is *first-degree* burn, which is also called *superficial* burn. Injury is of the epidermis or outermost skin layer.

Second-degree burn or *partial-thickness* burn is blistered and usually down into the dermis second layer. Since there is more blistering, there is more potential loss of fluid.

There is also *third-degree* or *full-thickness* burn, which may be down to the hypodermis, the deepest layer of the skin.

Sources for burns—Chemicals, heat, or cold may all cause burns to the skin or outer layers. In homeopathy, the etiology or cause is not as significant as the symptoms expressed.

Burn severity—It depends on the *depth* and the *total area of burns* that are affected on the body, the percentage of the body that's burned.

Symptoms of Each Type of Burn

First degree or superficial—There's redness, pain, and no blisters, and there's mild swelling.

Second degree or partial thickness—There's redness, blisters, pain, and more swelling.

Third degree or full thickness—The burn may appear black, it is deep, and often painless if deeper nerve layer is destroyed. Third degree is through the full-skin layer down to the deeper fascia, muscle, or bone. There's a great deal of infection risk with the second—and third-degree burns, and loss of fluid is another risk factor, depending on the surface area and depth of skin affected.

First-Degree or Superficial Burns

First aid treatment is usually cool water, which is standard at this time. Although some have tried warm water using the "like treats like" principle, I've found that that's worked. It may work as it allows the heat to be dispersed as the local blood vessels remain dilated and allow flow. When applying cold, there is vasoconstriction that may trap the heat to the cells injured, resulting in more injury at the site. The important thing is to clean the wound with water and provide comfort.

Lavender Oil—This oil as a topical soak has been comforting for some. This would be the herbal treatment.

Urtica Urens—Give 30C every 10 minutes for 1 hour, then less, using as needed. This works well for superficial burns because, sometimes, the superficial is a little prickly like you'd think of with the Urtica Urens rash.

Second-Degree or Partial Thickness Burns

First aid treatment: Again, treatment is cool water or "like treats like" with warm water.

Medical attention is often required because fluid replacement will be needed if there is a significant area burned. Tetanus should be updated if more than five years have passed since the last dose; burn cleansing and debridement (which is removing part) of open blisters and after which appropriate dressings are applied will also assist in healing.

Homeopathic Remedy Treatments

Aconite or Arnica—Use depending on their symptoms. Aconite, if they're very fearful; Arnica, if they're okay, but they're really not. So consider those two remedies as first line treatment.

Causticum—This would be the next treatment: 30C given every 10 minutes and that's for a burning pain or a very painful burn.

Kali Bichromicum—Give 30C for a deeper burn that's ulcerated or for a steam or vapor burn. It works well for a steam burn.

Third-Degree or Full Thickness Burns

Apply *first aid* and you may want to elevate the parts so there is not so much fluid loss; use cool water and clean dressing to protect the injured area. Get these folks to the emergency room since the risk of infection is high and the risk of shock and loss of fluids is also high.

Homeopathic Remedies

Consider shock remedies: **Aconite or Arnica**. Again, depending on the patient.

Aconite—They're very fearful.

Arnica—"I'm okay" when they aren't okay. Usually, giving a single dose helps.

Cantharis—Give 30C every 5 to 15 minutes for intense pain or if they're coming out of their skin from pain. Consider this for first—or second-degree burns if the symptoms fit.

Calendula—Give 200C, once for severe or large area burns, which will help with healing and infection that could result from the burn itself.

Chemical Burns

Carbolic Acid—It is that shock remedy; there's nausea, a dusky look to them, and they feel as if they're dying. They want to get into a cold bath; they're cold and wanting cold.

Causticum—It is for burns that are cracking or ulcerating or that fail to heal; they're better with cold drink, better washing and better with warmth of bed. So a burning with better warmth is Causticum.

Picric Acid—They're small painful blisters, very similar to a Picric Acid burn on the skin. It's burning pain, so they're better cold and they're better if they're covered up.

Cantharis—It gives intense pain. They feel as if they're coming out of their skin, and they are better with warmth and rest.

Apis—Chemical burns to the eyes or minor burns with marked pain, redness, and swelling. Consider Apis. They're better with cold, and again, this would the other symptom of Apis.

Sunburn

Urtica Urens—There is burning heat, some swelling, but more prickly burning heat. Consider Urtica Urens.

Cantharis—It is hot, burning, angry-looking, much pain, very uncomfortable symptoms with the sunburn that needs Cantharis.

Also consider topical treatments: Cantharis, Plantago (which helps with inflammation)**, Aloe Vera**, and **Hamamelis** (witch hazel). These are old-time treatments for sunburn that are available as herbal treatments and might be helpful to apply directly to the burned area.

Frostbite or Chilblains

Frostbite is from extreme cold, and there are many symptoms that are similar to a burn, and they can be superficial or partial or full-thickness injuries to the skin.

Homeopathic Remedies

Agaricus—It is the feeling of burning, itching, red, swelling, and is better with gentle motion.

Pulsatilla—The area of injury itches as it is reheating, and they are better carried or gentle motion. They like some air going by. That's Pulsatilla, the windflower.

Arsenicosum—There is much anxiety, there's much restlessness, there's marked pain and deep chill. There's blackened skin, and there's the threat of gangrene. Arsenicosum would be a great remedy to choose if those conditions are met.

Nitricum Acidum—These are old scars that are painful if cold; they're sticking, splintery pains. They are worse jarring and feel better with pressure. So consider that in the healing of chilblains, which have remaining sticking pains.

Crotalus Horridus—This burn has a blackness to the skin, there's marked swelling, there's gangrene that's going to sepsis. It's usually right sided but could be in either spot. This would be a Crotalus Horridus frostbite, which, if it doesn't heal, may need surgical intervention.

Open Wounds

First aid for open wounds: Give the *A, B, C,* and *D*s and to the emergency room as needed. Clean and cover the wound. If severe or if bleeding is not controlled, then further allopathic treatment is needed.

Incisions—These are a clean, sharp cut. If it's small, you can just clean with a Calendula tincture or ointment and just cover it up.

Homeopathic Remedies for Wounds

Staphysagria—If there's great pain along the new wound site, give 30C every 15 minutes.

Calendula—It is the next for healing. Use 30C twice a day and increase to 4 times a day if there are any red edges that develop. Calendula will both help heal the wound and decrease chance of infection.

If it's sutured, do not use any topical Calendula. Oral treatment is better as this allows the healing to begin from the inside out as opposed to the outside in which topical would be the outside in. So you must use internal dosing (oral) of Calendula if sutures are present.

Wounds: Abrasions

First aid: For common scrapes, clean and control the bleeding.

Homeopathic Treatment
Treat as above for incisions with **Staphysagria** or **Calendula.**

Topically: Also, apply tinctures of Hypericum if there's significant pain shooting out from the wound and Calendula for infection, and help with healing may be used. You can also mix together and dilute and place on dressing. You can get ointments or creams with both of these plants present. And you can take orally as a remedy. There are many choices for treating abrasions.

Wounds: Lacerations

First aid for lacerations: They may be jagged or tears in the skin, or they may be deep. The first need is to control the bleeding and to seek surgical repair if necessary.

Homeopathic Remedies

First, use **Arnica** or **Aconite** for shock. Again, the shock of Arnica—they'd be fine; the shock of Aconite—they're worried and restless and scared.

Hypericum—This is for severe nerve pain shooting out from the wound. Pain seems worse than the wound looks.

Staphysagria—It is for pain over the wound itself.

Calendula—Give 30C, 3 times a day for general healing; it will help the suture and wound heal and decrease the threat of infection. Not a bad plan!

Puncture Wounds

First aid—Medical attention to remove the object and update the tetanus shot

Homeopathic Treatment

Ledum—Give 30C, 3 times a day for healing. This is great for puncture wounds if they're cold and better cold.

Hypericum tincture—Apply topically to the dressing to help with pain that's shooting out from the wound, which is common. (Avoid Calendula topically because of the depth from the puncture wound. You want it to heal from the inside out, not the outside in.)

Hypericum—Give 30C, 4 times a day, stopping Ledum, if pain shoots up and out from the wound.

Dosage: If deep, infected wound to leg, consider Ledum 1M and then Calendula 30C to assist with the healing. And you'll find that it'll heal quite nicely and quickly. But treatment is needed depending on the depth and location. And they may need antibiotics in addition to the update of tetanus.

Contusions

Contusions are injuries usually resulting from blunt trauma to an area, and the skin is still intact, but you see discoloration as one would see in a bruise or tender swelling.

First Aid

A cold pack and compression may help. If the contusions are over vital structures, consider an emergency room visit, depending where injury occurred, e.g., as injured kidneys or spleen can result in severe complications and be life threatening.

Homeopathic Remedies

Arnica—Give 30C, 3-4 times a day. Start as soon as possible as the first remedy of choice and the most common remedy.

If the lesion is cold and numb, **Ledum** is a better choice. Cold and numb, better cold, consider Ledum instead of Arnica.

Ruta Graveolens—It is the bruise to the periosteum or shinbone. These are quite painful, but Ruta is the best remedy for that kind of bone bruise, as well as for shins and forearms by the elbow.

Bellis Perennis—This is for persistent bruising and outstanding soreness or for a pelvic area injury or for soft tissue with internal cyst within the bruise. Consider Bellis.

Sulphuricum Acidum—It is for persistent very sore, blue bruise.

Conium—If it's a breast or testicular injury that's a hard lump within the bruise, consider Conium. It's a great choice for that.

Dosing for bruises—Give 30C as needed for healing; it might be 3 times a day. It might take several days to heal things up.

Head Injury

First Aid

Remember *A, B, C, D*s if there is loss of consciousness or if there are other obvious neurologic changes, this person should be taken to an emergency room for more complete evaluation and perhaps head scans. All head injuries, even if slight concussion—nausea or headache or dizziness—should be monitored especially the first twenty-four hours to watch for any change in neurological function.

Homeopathic Remedies

Arnica—Give a high dose, frequently if it's severe and the patient says they're okay.

Nat Sulph—Give this if there's dizziness or concussion after a head injury.

Hypericum—Give this if there's headache and convulsions after a head injury. Remember, Hypericum is the nerve remedy so that would make sense as headache and convulsions would be nerve related.

Opium—This is for stupor or coma after a head injury.

Dosage
If severe or life threatening, 200C, 1M, or 10M—frequency depends on severity. If you only have a 30C, give it and repeat it often.

Sprains and Strains

Strains are injuries to muscles due to overexertion or overstretching.
Sprains involve soft tissue, tendons, ligaments—when wrenched too far past normal range of motion.

First Aid

Allopathically, it's usually RICE: Rest, ice, compression, and elevation

Homeopathically, RACE: rest, Arnica, compression, and elevation. Supportive care—first aid treatment if any other injuries.

X-rays may be needed to rule out fractures, so they may need to be seen, and you may need to evaluate for the situation that's occurring and what you see with the patient.

Homeopathic Remedies

Remedy of first choice: **Arnica,** 30C every hour times 5 doses and then every 6 hours for 12-24 hours to decrease the swelling and start the healing.

Then use symptoms for specific injury characteristics:

Bryonia—Give 30C for 4 times a day. This is pain with least motion and will be decided upon after you've treated with the acute remedy, Arnica.

Rhus Tox—Give 30C for 2 times a day for stiff pain in the morning or after rest. better with motion, but it fatigues late in the day if used a lot. It's worse in the cold and damp, better with heat. Consider Rhus Tox.

Ruta Graveolens—Give 30C for twice a day if the injury is close to the bone. A shin splint would likely respond well to Ruta Graveolens.

Calcarea Carbonica—For persistent weakness after the injury that should be well healed or if there is no clear picture after you've tried the other remedies, consider Calc Carb.

Millefolium—This remedy is great is for any Achilles tendon injury.

Arnica—If you feel beat-up or have an overused feeling or if you want cold compresses or if after a marathon, there's a general body, leg strain/sprain, then consider Arnica. If you run marathons and feel sore afterward, take Arnica 30C an hour before you run and repeat a dose after you're done. You might avoid that beat-up feeling.

Rhus Tox—They will want warmth on their strain. And again, it is worse at first movement and better after a bit of movement, but they tire easily.

Hypericum—This is a nerve-pain remedy; if there's sciatic shooting pains after a spinal tap or tailbone injury kind of strain, consider Hypericum.

Bryonia—If there's sharp, stabbing or aching pains and worse with the least movement, better put pressure on the part to immobilize it. Ninety percent of muscle strains are Bryonia strains. It's a great remedy to have on hand.

Bone Fractures

First Aid Treatment

Avoid moving if there is spinal cord injury unless they are in danger with where they are positioned, e.g., in the middle of a highway or in a burning car. An additional note: ask them if it's okay to move them before you move them. If they're unconscious, then that's a decision you'll have to make to keep them safe. Apply *A, B, C, D*s of first aid. Injured-part immobilization and take to physician's office / urgent care / emergency room for x-rays and medical treatment as necessary.

Homeopathic Remedies

Bach's RESCUE Remedy—If it's available, it's a great choice. Just give them a few drops right away on the tongue and repeat as necessary.

Arnica—Give Arnica for shock or bruising, **Aconite** if they're very fearful. Give either one of those first.

Bryonia—It is very helpful to give before the bone is set. Why do you think that is? Because pain is worse with least movement. If you have a broken bone, any movement hurts until it's in good position, so Bryonia is a great remedy to give before setting the bone. Then it doesn't need to be repeated, usually.

After the Bone Is Set: Some Remedies to Use
Symphytum—Give 30C, 3 times a day for 10 days to 2 weeks. It can be used daily for 1 week and then weekly while in cast. The other way to take Symphytum is to take it 3 times a day until you notice there's not an ache at the point of the fracture, and that usually is within 10 to 14 days and then stop. That means the callus has been formed and the bone is healing well. Based on personal experience, I have found that Symphytum almost cuts the bone healing in half of the time typically needed. Most bones heal within 4 to 6 weeks although some are a bit longer and also depend on age.

Compound Fractures

Consider **Hypericum** or **Calendula** according to the case.

Hypericum if there's pain shooting from the wound or intensive nerve pain.

Calendula if there's chance of infection and then take it 3 times a day until the symptoms improve.

Eupatorium Perfoliatum—It is for bone-breaking pain. Take 30C, 2 to 3 times a day for 2-3 days and follow that with Symphytum. Eupatorium would be used before you'd use Symphytum and would greatly help with pain relief.

Sulphuric Acid—It is for the deep bruising pain that remains; the bone pain is gone, but it feels bruised, and it is especially good for the *tailbone area.*

Slow Healing or Persisting Pain
If they're slow-healing bones or if the pain is persisting:

Calc Carb if there's nonunion or the pain lasts for two weeks with the cast. It assists the callus.

Calc Phos is for nonunion fractures.

Calc Sulph for the feeling of instability at the fracture site after things supposedly have healed. Consider any of those, 30C, 3 times a day until they feel better.

Bryonia—It is for injured or *fractured ribs* with pain in breathing. Remember, Bryonia is for pain with least movement; there's no way to splint the ribs. Bryonia is a great remedy for a pleuritic pain, especially fracture, but as discussed, it is for pleuritic pain with lung infections.

Presurgery Remedies

Aconite—It is to be taken if there's a great fear of death, presurgery, or they're very *nervous or anxious* about surgery. This is best taken the *night before.* It will help you sleep. It's also a great remedy to use before the dental visit for those who are very *dental phobic.*

Day-of-Surgery Remedies

Arnica—It can be used before surgery; give 200C or 1M, 1 hour before and use afterward for pain and bruising. It's a great help. Sometimes, one doesn't need a narcotic if they use Arnica with a Tylenol or ibuprofen.

Presurgery—Avoid vitamin E, omega-3s, aspirins, nonsteroidals for at least one week before the surgery to decrease bleeding and bruising around the surgical site. That will assist with healing because all those things thin the blood.

After-Surgery Remedies

- **Aurum**—Postoperatively there's a real sense of gloom, doom, black mood, don't touch me—this is the sense an Aurum person will have. We need to be touched many times postoperatively. They'll take vitals as often as every five to fifteen minutes. An Aurum would be very uncomfortable with that, and if you give them Aurum 30C on waking postsurgery, they wouldn't have that sense of discomfort.
- **Bismuth Metallicum**—If there's much vomiting postoperatively, 30C as soon as they waken probably can forgo the vomiting upon waking up. This can happen despite some of the perioperative meds given to decrease vomiting. Bismuth is a great one to have on hand. Just a tablet and vomiting is gone. It can prevent rehospitalization due to dehydration especially if it's a same-day surgery.
- **Calendula**—Consider this remedy for heart, chest surgery, for mastectomy. Calendula is a great remedy for removal of organs. Calendula helps with healing for these situations. (See Wounds)
- **Bellis Perennis**—It is most useful for trauma to soft organs, either from the surgery or the reason for the surgery, especially involving the *liver*, *spleen*, *uterus*, or *breast*. Bellis is a great treatment if trauma has occurred either perioperatively or preoperatively or is the reason for needing surgery.
- **Calendula or Coffea**—It is for severe stump pain after amputation.
- **Phosphorus**—It is for extreme fear of surgery and for excessive bleeding during or after surgery. This is great for a tooth extraction. Give 30C every 15 minutes until the bleeding stops or if there is a lot of bleeding after the tooth extraction or other surgery.
- **Staphysagria**—It is for pain or infection at the sight of the incision. If they're freaking out about it, there's real agony, their stomach is upset, consider Staphysagria. You can give a 200C or 1M—even 30C—if that's all you have since it's pretty superficial. If the emotional freaking out is there, 200C would be better, but if it's superficial infection or pain along the incision, consider Staphysagria 30C.
- **Hypericum**—This remedy is for shooting nerve pain or persistent numbness around the incision. It's also great for dental work where's there's persistent numbness and shooting pain from either injection

of Novocain or the extraction or the previous tooth injury that caused the need for dental work. Consider Hypericum.

Dosage: For all these postsurgical remedies, consider 30C as needed for discomfort. Stop as soon as better.

Mastectomy Remedies

- **Arnica**—It is for soreness and bruising around mastectomy.
- **Bellis Perennis**—To be taken if the soreness is greatly increased and there's much injury or bruising.
- **Staphysagria**—To be taken if there is stinging incisional pain. Consider using it postmastectomy.

Review Quiz

1. What is the major difference in using Arnica or Aconite in acute injury?
2. When would you use Calendula orally as a remedy versus topically for wounds?
3. What remedy do you think of for acute injury with shooting pain, in the eye or head, finger or nerve injury?
4. When is it time to consider another remedy?
5. What are some benefits of plussing, and how do you do it?
6. When is it time to seek other help?
7. Can allopathic and homeopathic treatments be used together? Please explain.

(Answers are on page 76.)

Answer to Quizzes

Introduction to Homeopathy

1. Like treats like.
2. Remedy is a substance that is diluted and energized to encourage healing.
3. Miasm is a way to classify disease to choose remedies and is similar to family traits or inheritance.
4. Samuel Hahnemann is the father of homeopathy.
5. Disease is a body imbalance and attempt to attain best health with symptoms from that imbalance being part of the disease.
6. $30C = 1/100^{30}$, $10X = 1/10^{10}$ dilutions.
7. Succussion is pounding the remedy or stirring to energize the substance being diluted.

Homeopathy for Acute Illness

1. Aconite
2. Arsenicosum
3. Apis Mellifica
4. Bryonia Alba
5. Lachesis
6. Calc Carb (worse cold or change of weather) or Pulsatilla (left-sided, worse in heat, better if carried, gentle motion, or open air)
7. UTI

    A. Pain—Cantharis (scalding, better cold, better emptying)
    B. Frequency—Nux Vomica (constant, full sensation)
    C. Pain at end of urination—Sarsaparilla (copious urine)

    D. UTI post coition—Staphysagria (bladder spasm during, after completion)

    E. Urine Scanty—Apis (burning, better cold)

    F. Retention of urine in newborn or woman after labor—Aconite (fright and cold)

Homeopathy for First Aid—Part I

1. Airway, breathing, circulation, dial or dispatch—call 911.
2. False—we need both homeopathy and allopathic care at times.
3. Apis Mellifica
4. Bryonia Alba
5. Acute injury

    A. Arnica Montana
    B. Arsenicosum Album
    C. Aconite

Homeopathy for First Aid—Part II

1. Arnica—Everything is fine, bleeding, and bruising versus Aconite—"I am going to die" and they are really scared and restless.
2. Calendula (topical or oral)—The depth of the wound—you want to heal from the inside out, not the outside in. Use orally if it's deep and with stitches, and topically if it's superficial and no stitches.
3. Hypericum Perfoliatum
4. After giving (3, if severe problem) 6 doses, if nothing is helping, reconsider and retake the case to see if there's a better remedy to choose.
5. Plussing will increase the dose of a remedy. If you have only a few pellets, you can stretch them out over a day or more with 1, 2, or 3 pellets in a quarter cup of filtered or distilled water, stir it 10 times, and take a teaspoon for each dose. Stir 10 times before each dose. Use a glass and metal teaspoon.
6. Any severe injury or anytime you would need assistance, you should seek help. If there's no improvement or if there's a worsening of symptoms, it's appropriate to get help from other sources. Time and severity determine when one should seek assistance.
7. Allopathic and homeopathic methods can work well together. However, there are some limitations as one can nullify the other, but they also can assist each other nicely.

Where to Order Remedies

Helios Pharmacy (sells kits)
97 Cameden Road
Trunbridge Wells
Kent TN1 2QR www.helios.co.uk

Hahnemann Laboratories
1940 Fourth Street
San Rafael, CA 94901
888-427-6422 www.hahnemannlabs.com

360 Homeopathy
1609 W. Babcock, Suite G
Bozeman, MT 59715
406-582-5499
Remedies360@yahoo.com

Boiron USA
6 Campus Boulevard
Newtown Square, PA 19073
800-258-8823 www.boironusa.com

Also, locate your local whole foods or cooperative store, which often sell
homeopathic remedies.

Index

CPSIA information can be obtained at www.ICGtesting.com
Printed in the USA
LVOW062018211212

312654LV00002B/130/P